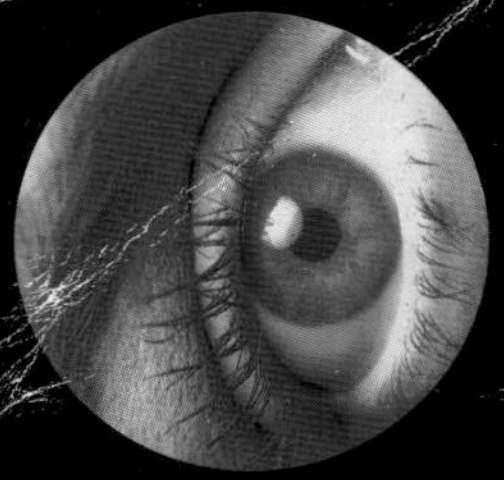

N.Y. GOLD

OLUME
8

President
Arie Kopelman

Chairman of the Board
Ira Shapiro

Associate Publisher
Jane Flanagan

Production Director
David Spector

Traffic
Neal Hemphill

Sales Representative: Photography
Franny O'Gorman

Sales Representative: Creative Services
Robyn Selman

Cover & Tab Design
Kama Design +

Typesetting
V & M Graphics

Color Separations
Daiichi Graphic Systems Co. Ltd.
Hong Kong

Printing & Binding
Everbest Printing Co. Ltd.
Hong Kong

Photo Credits

Front Cover
© Brad Guice (flower)
Tab 1, Pages 2-3; Tab 2, Pages 90-91
© Gary Goldberg (woman)
Tab 1, Page 24
© Bob London (eye)
Tab 1, Pages 20-21; Tab 2, Pages 102-103
© Ellen Silverman (fries)
Tab 2, Page 81
© Douglas Rosa (faucet)
Tab 2, Pages 46-47
© Alan Kaplan (couple)
Tab 1, Pages 133-148

Back Cover
© Rob Lang (backflip)
Tab 1, Pages 108-109
© Dennis Galante (clock)
Tab 2, Pages 36-39
© Heungman (man)
Tab 1, Page 73
© Paul Armbruster (glasses)
Tab 2, Pages 146-147
© Bob London (eye)
Tab 1, Pages 20-21; Tab 2, Pages 102-103
© John Bean (boys)
Tab 1, Page 8

Tab 1
© Dennis Milbauer
Tab 1, Page 107
Tab 2
© Bill Milne
Tab 2, Pages 122-123
Tab 3
© Eric Huang
Tab 2, Pages 62-63

Published By
New York Gold, Inc.
10 East 21st Street
New York, N.Y. 10010
Telephone: (212) 254-1000
Fax: (212) 254-1204

N.Y. Gold
ISBN: 1-882202-09-0

For Sales Outside U.S.
Rotovision S.A.
9, Route Suisse
CH - 1295 - Mies
Switzerland
Telephone: 22-755-30-55
Fax: 22-755-40-72

Table of Contents

1

Tab 1
Photography

People

2

Tab 2
Photography

Still Life
Interiors
Food

3

Tab 3
Listings & Advertisers
Photo Services

Photographer Listings
Photography Representative Listings

LUCIANA PAMPALONE STUDIO
212-564-2883
448 WEST 37th STREET, #9E • NEW YORK, NEW YORK 10018

PREMIERE

PUEBLO INDIANS

RCA RECORDS

COCA-COLA / MCCANN-ERICKSON

BRAD GUICE

212.941.6096

232 WEST BROADWAY NYC 10013

REPRESENTED BY

JANICE MOSES

212.779.7929

The New York Times

Toyota / Saatchi & Saatchi

AT&T

Traver Company

LEDDY
LEDDY'S

Brad Guice

212.941.6096

232 West Broadway NYC 10013

Represented by

Janice Moses

212.779.7929

VOLKMANN

The lasting moisture of Lubriderm.®
Lubriderm Lotion
Because your basic instinct is to save your skin.

JORDACHE

REPRESENTED BY LIZ-LI 212-889-7067

REUBEN NJAA

(nah)

TEXAS
210.271.0630

VICKI PRENTICE ASSOCIATES INC.
310.826.1332 • fax 310.284.3290

VICKI PRENTICE ASSOCIATES INC.
310.826.1332 • fax 310.284.3290

REUBEN NJAA

(nah)

TEXAS
210.271.0630

J O H N

BEAN

TEL 212 242-8106 FAX 212 691-8254 REP SUSAN O'GORMAN 212 645-6074

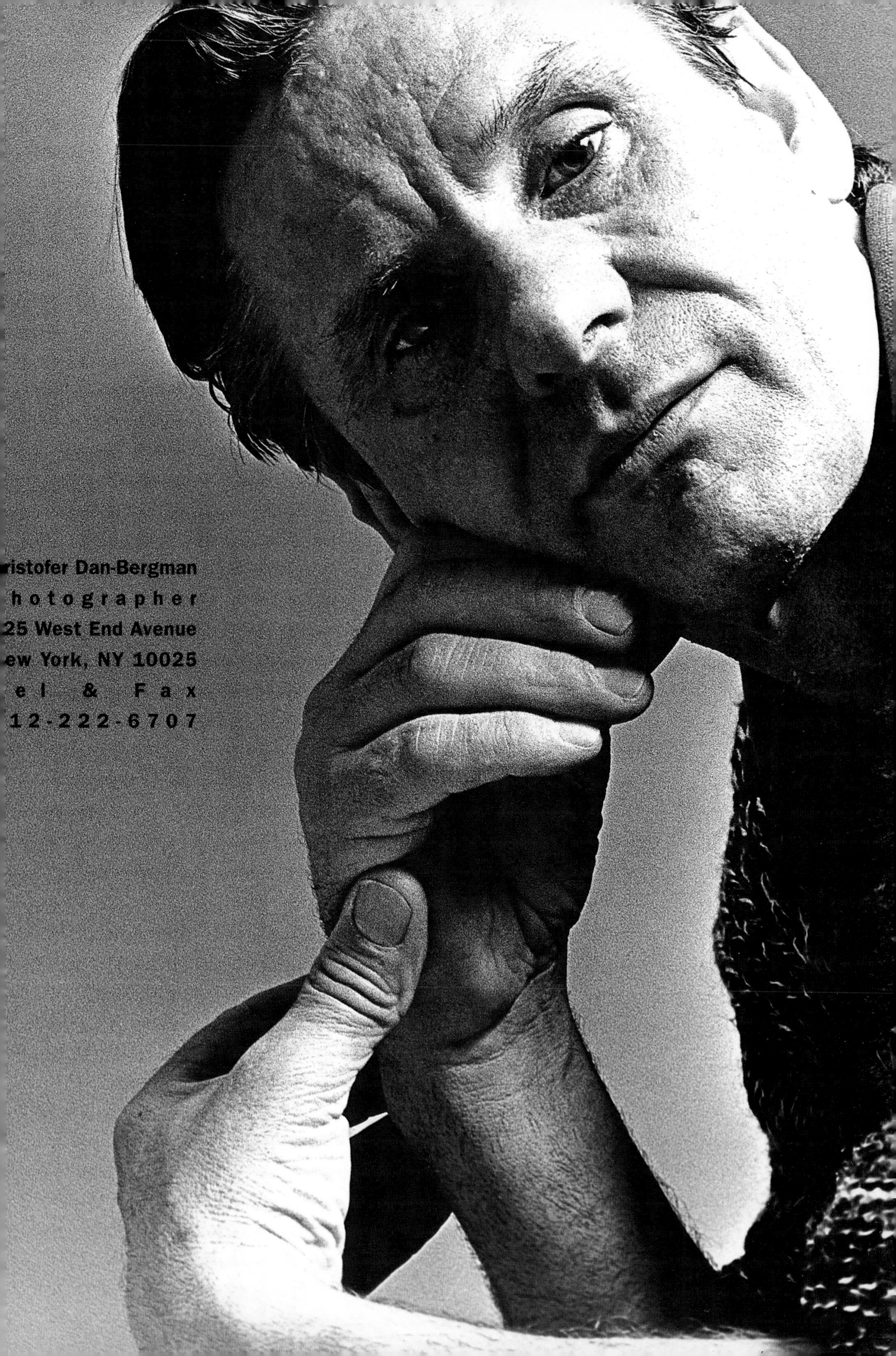
ristofer Dan-Bergman
hotographer
25 West End Avenue
ew York, NY 10025
el & Fax
12-222-6707

Telephone
CLAM

CLAM
BAR
Fish 'n' Chips

LEE PAGE 212·233·2227
REPRESENTED
N CHICAGO: JOSH HAIMS 312.939.5143

CLAM
BAR

LEE PAGE
212·233·2227
68 THOMAS ST. NY, NY 10013 • FAX 212.233.9128
REPRESENTED IN CHICAGO BY JOSH HAIMS • 312.939.5143

British GQ

ANTOINE VERGLAS

Mike Reinhardt
IMPRESSION PYTHON
Jean en coton (Cimarron, 390 F, aux Galeries Lafayette).

voyance en direct
YAGUEL DIDIER
se surpasse
ypnotisons-les avec la
MODE SERPENT
CUISINE A MARSEILLE
pas la politique
a vraie)
Qui? Avec qui?
101 potins à ne pas

Elle

MIKE REINHARDT

represented by Jean Gabriel Kauss • 212 779-4440 • Fax 725-0013

GILLES BENSIMON

Chen up: With three movies opening this year, Asian beauty Joan Chen has Hollywood by the horns. Dress by Richard Tyler. Hair: Cemal. Makeup: Francesca Tolot.

Demi Moore

LANCE STAEDLER

epresented by Jean Gabriel Kauss • 212 779-4440 • Fax 725-0013

Per il corpo cure particolari
Protezione assoluta è la parola d'ordine per il corpo che si avvicina al sole. E proprio una protezione assoluta è quella che sa assicurargli Ecran Hydro-Proterteur IP 12 della linea solare Stendhal. È un latte, leggero e assorbibile, che favorisce l'abbronzatura prevenendo, al tempo stesso, l'invecchiamento cutaneo grazie alla presenza dei fitosomi. Queste microsfere di origine naturale, che caratterizzano tutti i prodotti della gamma, contengono estratti di semi d'uva che vengono ma mano liberati per offrire alla pelle un azione anti-radicali liberi e un bel colore.

Se l'abbronzatura è a tutto movimento
Movimento, agilità, dinamismo: la tintarella è anche questo. Il prodotto per chi non desidera un rapporto statico col sole? Fresh Tanning Gel SPF 2, della linea solari Trussardi Action Sun. Freschissimo e gradevole, Fresh Tanning Gel è rivolto a tutte quelle pelli già scure, o poco sensibili, che non temono le esposizioni. Grazie alla sua consistenza e alla sua formula priva di sostanze grasse, questo specifico è l'abbronzante su misura per coloro che fanno sport anche in spiaggia e che quindi hanno bisogno di un prodotto non «invadente». (Canotta Dolce & Gabbana, mutande alte con bretelle Il Mare di Dolce & Gabbana).

ISABEL SNYDER

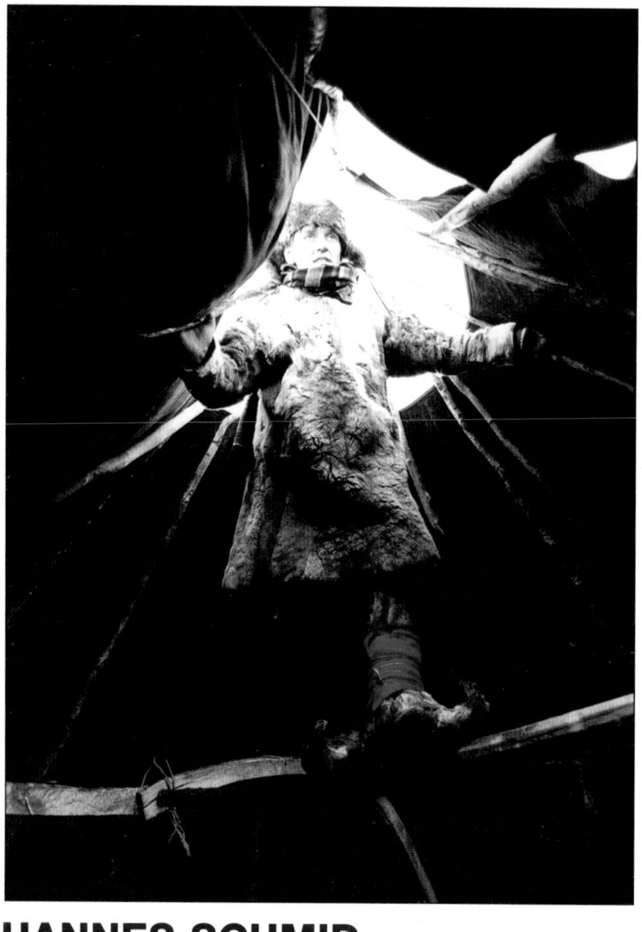

HANNES SCHMID

represented by Jean Gabriel Kauss • 212 779-4440 • Fax 725-0013

Die Mode im Zeichen der neuen Natürlichkeit zeigt viel Haut – und Mut zur Körperlichkeit
KÖRPER
BEWUSST
SEIN
Des Sommers schönste Kleider – teils Objekt, teils Kleidungsstück. Das Kleid aus reinem Seidenstrick (Martine Sitbon) betont die Figur nach allen Regeln der Kunst – durch Streifen und Fäden

RANÇOIS HALARD

OHN SCARISBRICK

epresented by Jean Gabriel Kauss • 212 779-4440 • Fax 725-0013

JONNIE MILES 212-865-7956

DENNIS BOURKE

Voyage

ORIGINAL
photography

COMPUTER
illustration

212·741·3211

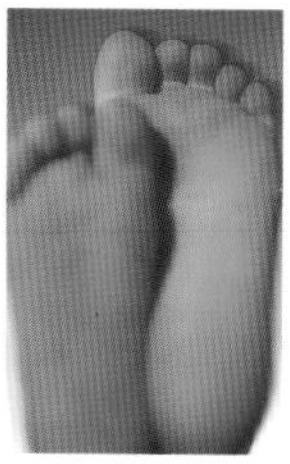

JOHN FORTUNATO

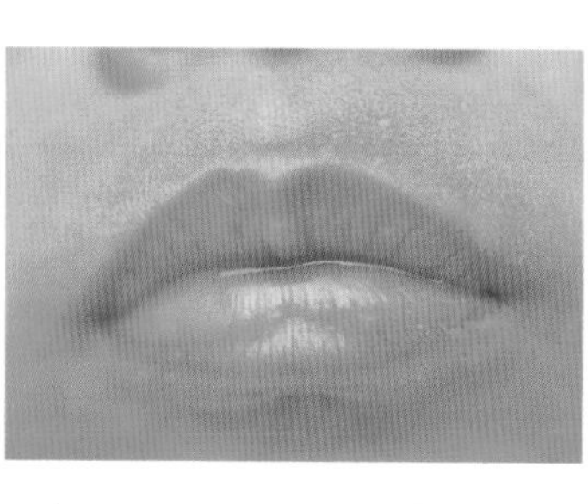

phone 212·620·7873   fax 212.620.7960

musicians, actors, performance artists, cowgirls, bodybuilders, portraits, fashion, advertisin

tors, performance artists, cowgirls, bodybuilders, portraits,

artists, advertising, editorial, fashion

musicians, actors, performance artists, cowgirls, bodybuilders, portraits

cowgirls, bodybuilders

[Bob LONDON]

[212] 966 4894

PHOTOGRAPHY

portraits, editorial, advertising,

cowgirls, bodybuilders

advertising,

JIRAIR AVEDIS
252 WEST 30th ST. #3
NEW YORK, N.Y. 100
212-244-3605

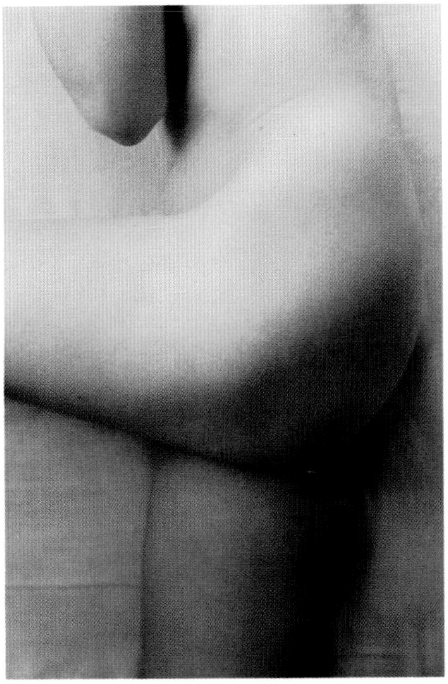

Cyndy Warwick New York City 212·420·4760

GARY GOLDBERG
photography

212 228 4820
voice
533 7013
fax-modem

LUCILLE
KHORNAK
212·593·0933
Stock Available

Johnson & Johnson
Alfa Romeo
Seiko
Givenchy
Sara Lee Corp.

SUZANNE OPTON

52 Broadway, New York, New York 10012 (212) 254-0372 Fax: (212) 260-9043

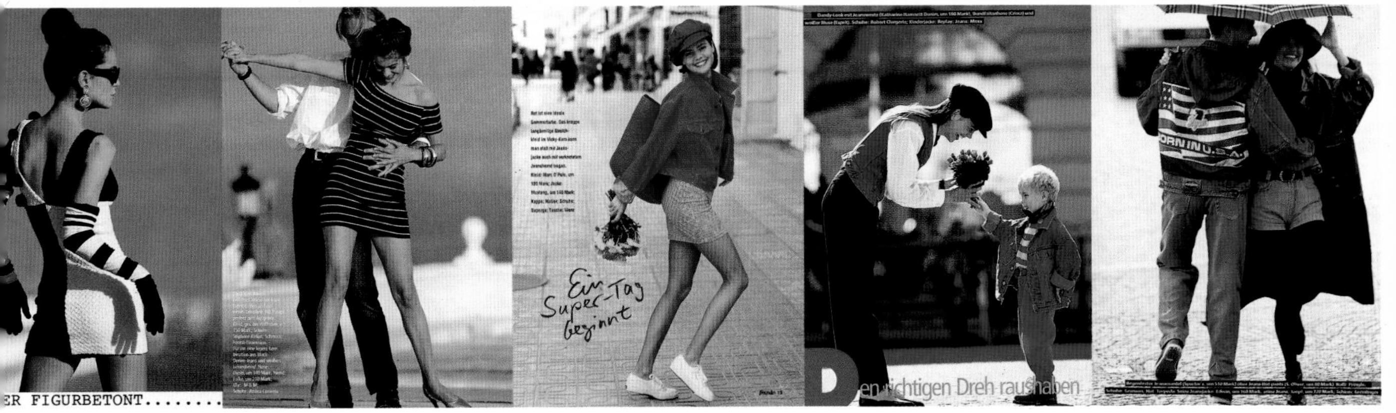
ER FIGURBETONT........
Ein Super-Tag beginnt
Den richtigen Dreh raushaben

NICOLAYSEN

PHOTOGRAPHY

DEN KÖRPER RICHTIG AUF TRAB BRINGEN
Tempo
Zu zweit auf Touren kommen

448 WEST 37TH STREET 12A NY, NY 10018
TEL: 212-947-5167 FAX: 212-268-6764

REPRESENTED BY CORINNE KARR

il paltò? nei toni cammello
Einsteigen bitte!
So kommen Sie
überall bestens an

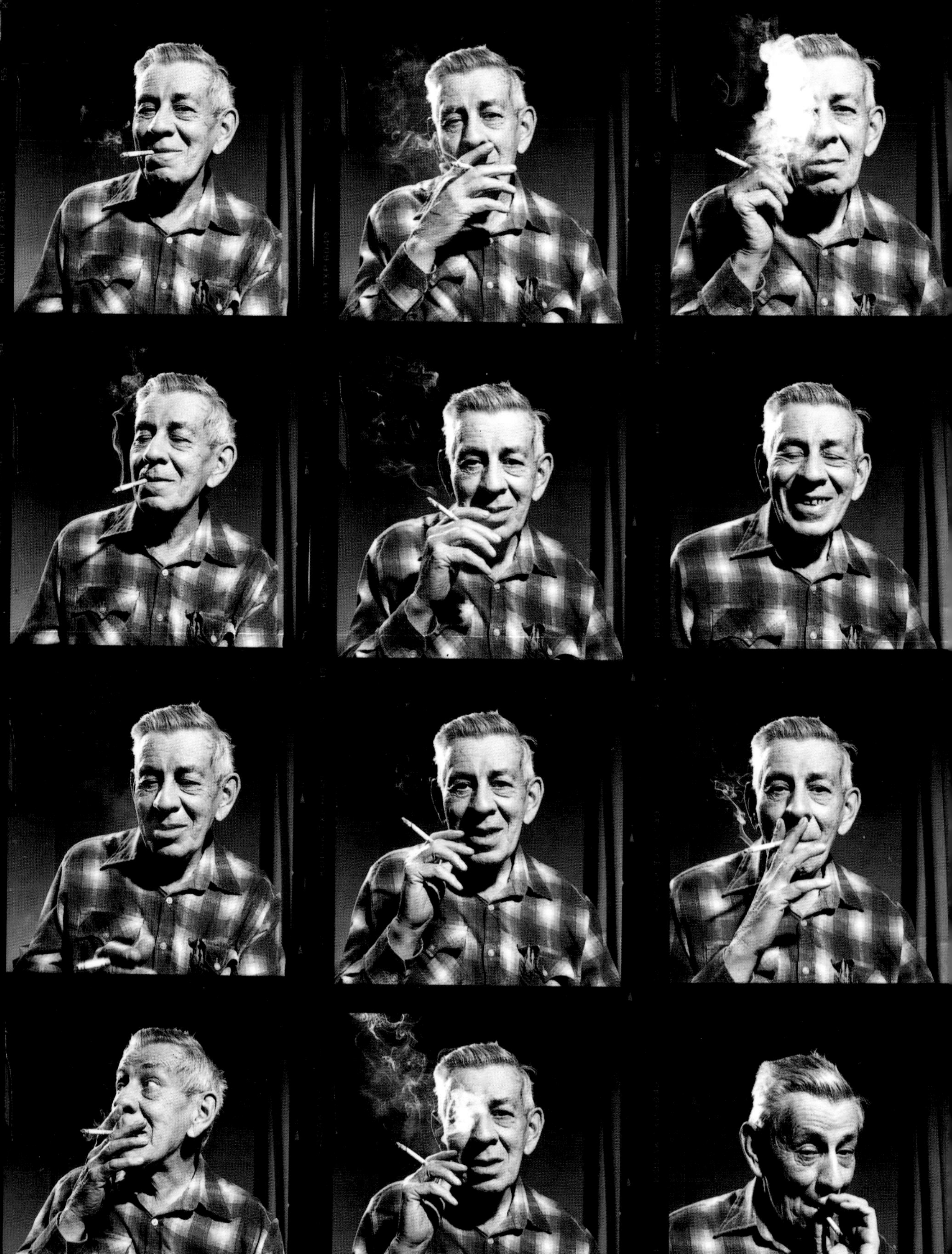

Jan Cobb

5 West 19
NYC 10011
(212) 255 - 1400
Fax: 627 - 1962

PENNY
GENTIE
380 LAFAYET
NYC 10003
212 475 445

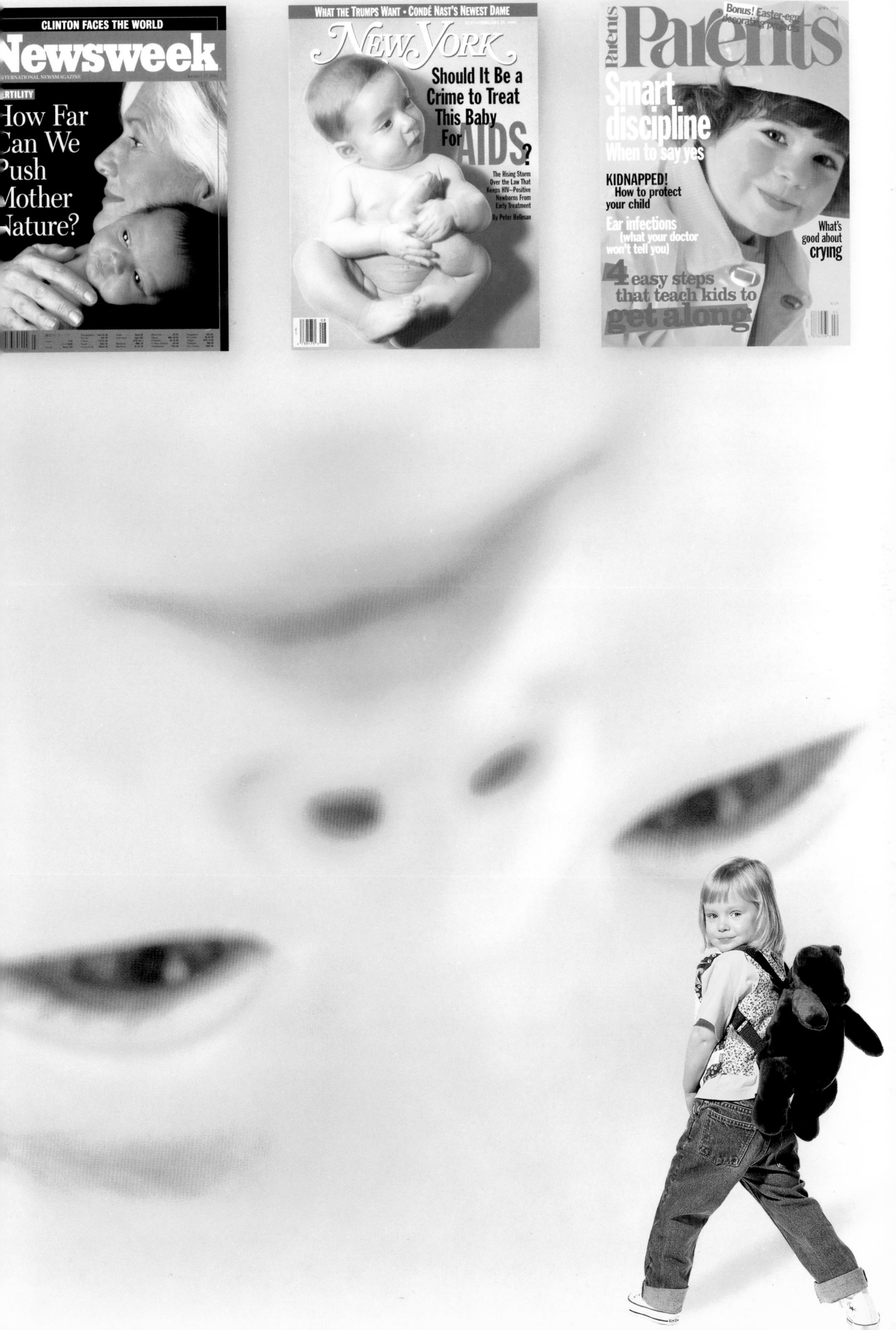
CLINTON FACES THE WORLD
Newsweek
TERNATIONAL NEWSMAGAZINE
ERTILITY
ow Far
an We
ush
lother
ature?
WHAT THE TRUMPS WANT • CONDÉ NAST'S NEWEST DAME
New York
Should It Be a Crime to Treat This Baby For AIDS?
The Rising Storm Over the Law That Keeps HIV-Positive Newborns From Early Treatment
By Peter Hellman
Parents
Bonus! Easter-egg decorating projects
Smart discipline
When to say yes
KIDNAPPED! How to protect your child
Ear infections (what your doctor won't tell you)
What's good about crying
4 easy steps that teach kids to get along

Tom Fogliani

212 620-0544
Represented by Cornelia Artist Representative

N

Advertising / Editorial / Corporate

JOSEPH A. ROSEN

326 W22 nd Street, #3R, New York, N.Y. 10011

Tel / Fax: 212 . 691 . 0607

N

PAUL GELSOBELLO PHOTOGRAPHY

245 West 29th Street, Studio 1200, New York, N.Y. 10001 **212.947.0317**

ANGELO CAGGIANO

212 - 463 - 0042

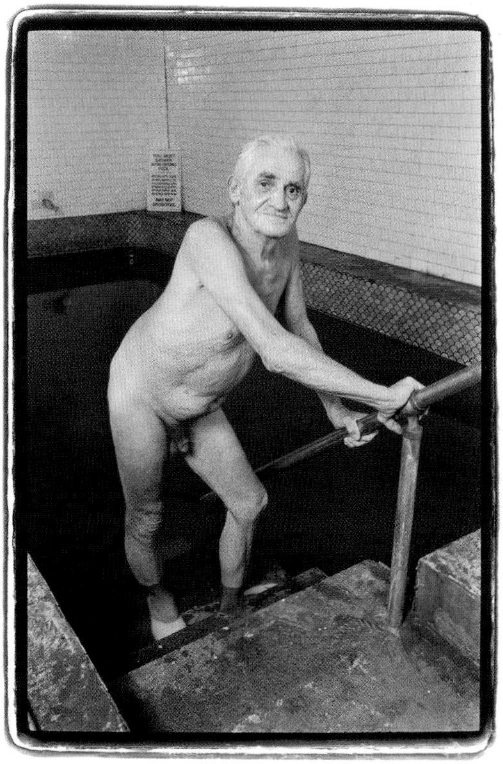

Sidney Weiner, attendent, Tenth Street Baths

CYCLONE

Eddie Day, brakeman, Cyclone Roller Coaster

Tom Rella, gravedigger

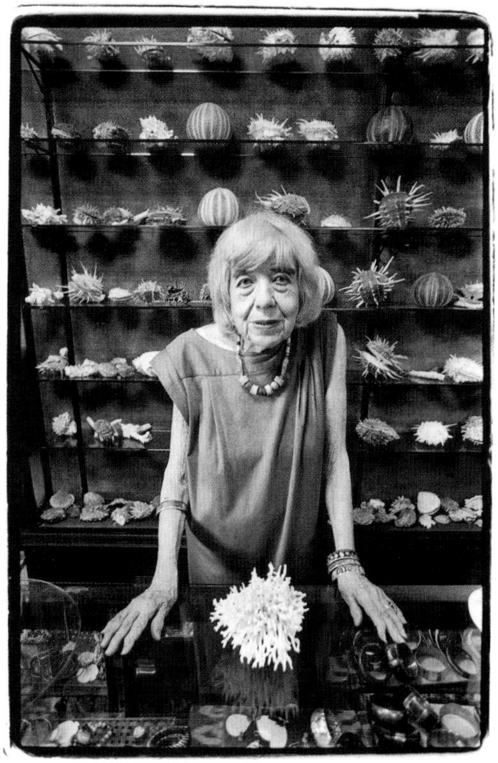

Veronica Parker Johns, owner, seashell shop

HARVEY WANG

REPRESENTED BY FLORENCE SILLEN (212) 243-9490

BRANDT
(212) 242-4289

A R M A

ARMA

Tom Arma, 38 West 26th Street, New York, N Y 10010
Represented by Adrienne Rubin, 212·243·7904

PAUL FREDRICK
MENSTYLE

Jean-Pierre Bonin
212-229-0426

PHOTOGRAPHER

JOE POLILLIO PHOTOGRAPHY 212·727·7450

REPRESENTED BY CHELSEA PHOTOGRAPHICS, INC BRIAN MOLLIN 212-695-5010

Elegant Bride
Elegant Bride June/July 1994 117

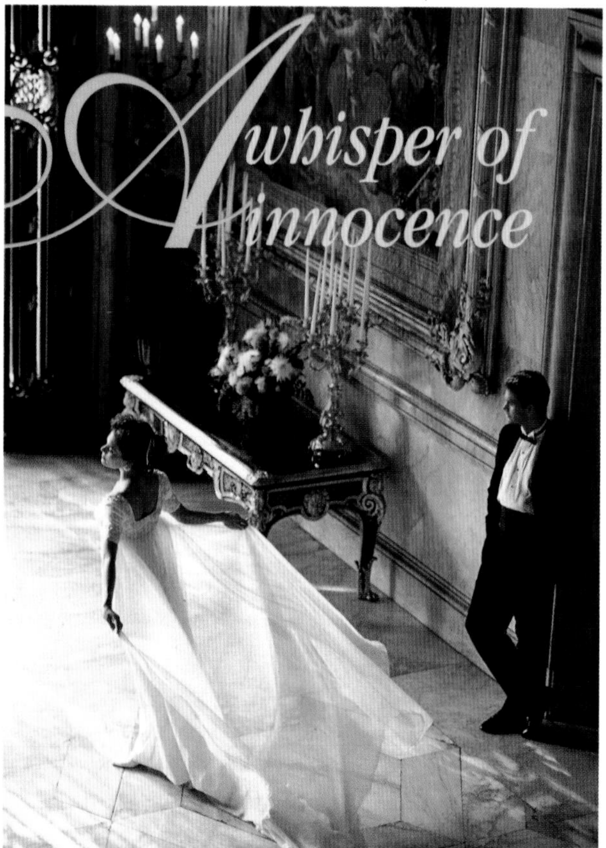
A whisper of innocence

© 1994 JOE POLILLIO

Lois Greenfield

CALL JOHN HENRY (212) 686·6883

Heidi Niemala

212/603-9817

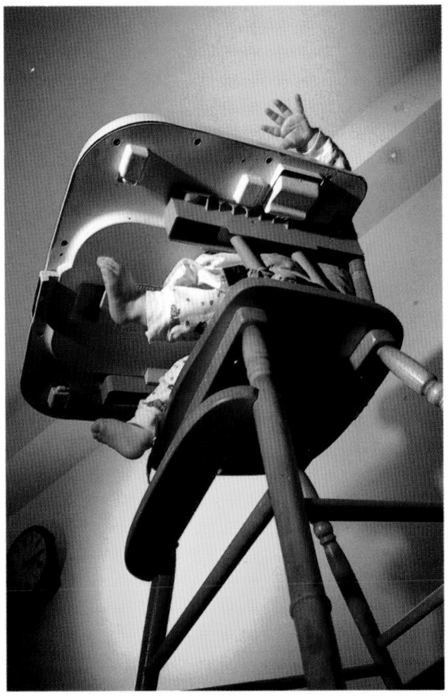

Calvin Klein
102

blunt cut looks
d on hair that is
ned up loosely
d styled with a
de tooth comb.

FUC
THE
WORL

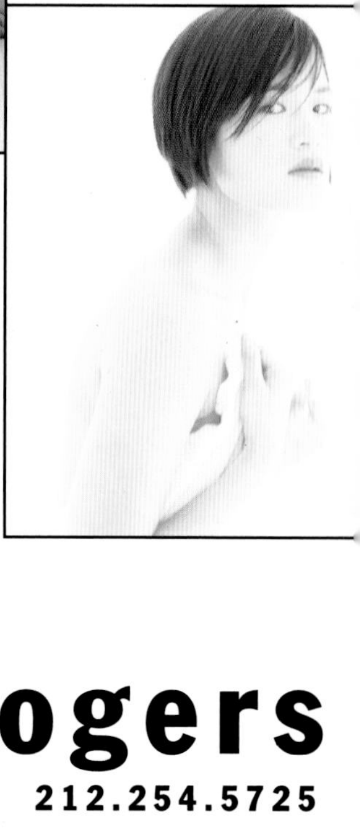

Chris M. Rogers

Represented by Robert Bacall 212.254.5725

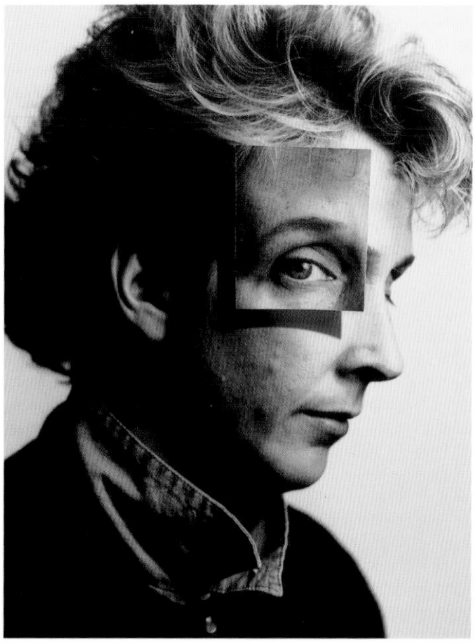

CHRIS JONES 212 685-0679

TIFFANY & CO.

CHRIS JONES 212 685-0679

ame
rica

photos by chris callis contact: marzena 212. 772 2522

ame
rica

H E U N G M A N

P H O T O G R A P H Y

2 1 2 • 2 2 8 • 2 8 8 2

DAVID KATZENSTEIN

ENTREE
212·529·9460
140

PULL

DAVID KATZENSTEIN

ENTREE
212·529·9460
140
TANGER

Julie Gang

NEW YORK CITY 212 925 3351 CONSULTANT DOREEN GEBBIA 212 388 2604

ROD COOK

2 0 3   8 3 8   2 8 5 5

GUESS LEATHER

GUESS LEATHER

GRANDE COLLECTION

LORD WEST

GUESS LEATHER

REPRESENTED ≺ bina ≻ 212 533 1734

ROD COOK

203 838 2855

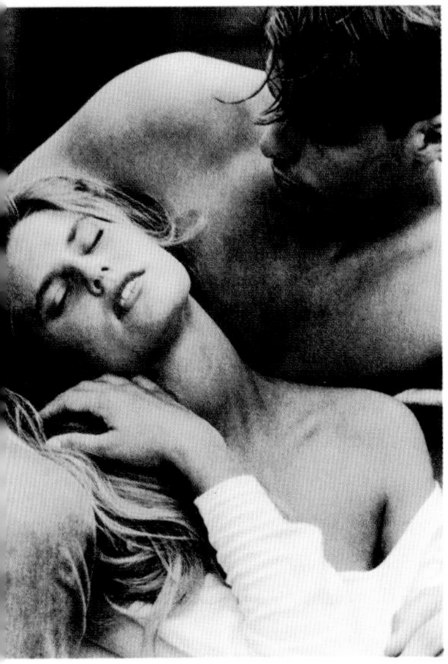

LORD WEST

LE COQ SPORTIF

GUESS LEATHER

REPRESENTED < bina > 212 533 1734

DAVID

(DR.)

WOOD

NEW YORK

REPRESENTED BY ZOLTAN 212.675.7696

C R E S T O

Alan Cresto · Represented by Levin Dorr 212 627-9871

ARIEL SKELLEY

PHOTOGRAPHY
212/226/4091

☆

REPRESENTED BY
LEVIN·DORR
212/627/9871

SPACE SHUTTLE

ARIEL SKELLEY

PHOTOGRAPHY
212/226/4091

☆

REPRESENTED BY
LEVIN·DORR
212/627/9871

kip meyer.

new york · 212 · 683 · 9039
milano · 02 · 331 · 053 · 51
paris · 1 · 48 · 87 · 57 · 40

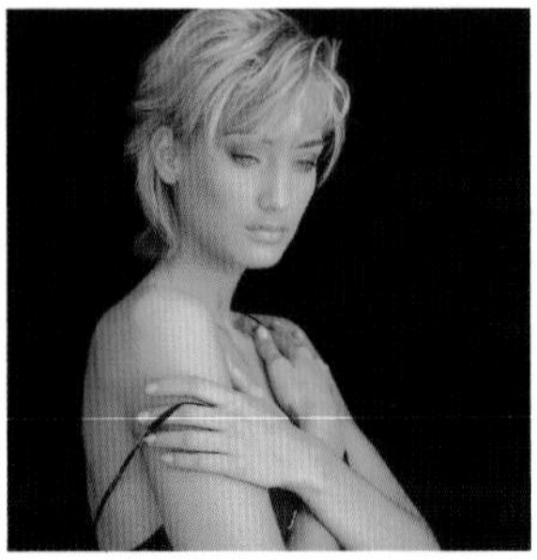

Ιστορία από βελούδο
ΜΟΔΑ
Μακρύ βελούδινο φόρεμα με τιράντες κάτω από εφαρμοστό σακάκι από κρουστό βελούδο 85.500 δρχ. Miss Coco. Βελούδινο καπέλο Ritch Bitch. Μπότες στρατιωτικές από το Μοναστηράκι. Καλσόν Belinda Negro, λίκρα, ματ, ψιλό και μονοκόμματο.

A sinistra, gilet impermeabile con cappuccio nascosto, Henry Cotton's, 140 mila lire circa; pullover Lupo di Mare-Malerba; pantaloni Henry Cotton's. A destra, blouson con cappuccio, Khatarine Hamnett, 190 mila lire circa; pantaloni Touche.
Vacanza è anche una giornata di mare sul vecchio gozzo, un pomeriggio sulla spiaggia a rammendare le reti, una pesca fortunata in alto mare, una serata tranquilla in porto
TEMPO LIBERO: PESCATORI E MARINAI
di Isabella Spada - foto di Beth Bischoff

LANVIN Studio
THE GREIF COMPANIES

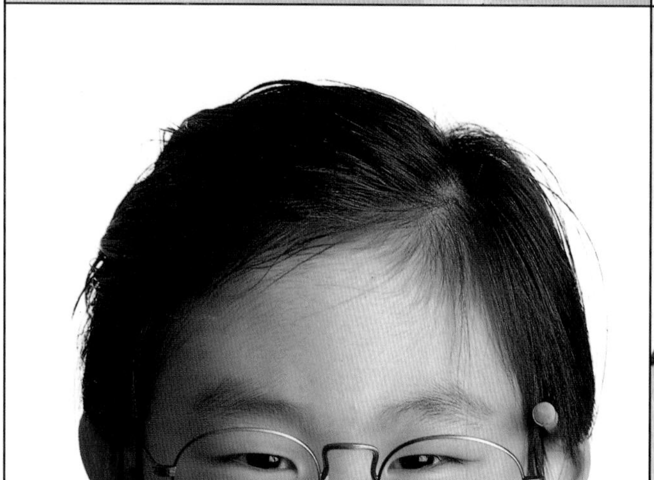

JOHN GIBBEL

JOHN GIBBEL PHOTOGRAPHY

SPIRAL PRODUCTIONS
212 802 8731

JOAN ELLEN THOMAS
PHOTOGRAPHY

180 EAST 79th STREET NEW YORK, NY 10021 212 794-9060 FAX 212 794-9110

ANDY FELDMAN

212•755•2630

JOHN • F • COOPER
212.545.0375

BACK STAGE

DAVID HAUTZIG PHOTOGRAPHY

209 East 25th Street • New York, NY 10010
212•779•1595

David also photographs Interiors. Turn to the Still Life section.

DAVID HAUTZIG PHOTOGRAPHY

209 East 25th Street • New York, NY 10010
212•779•1595

David also photographs Interiors. Turn to the Still Life section.

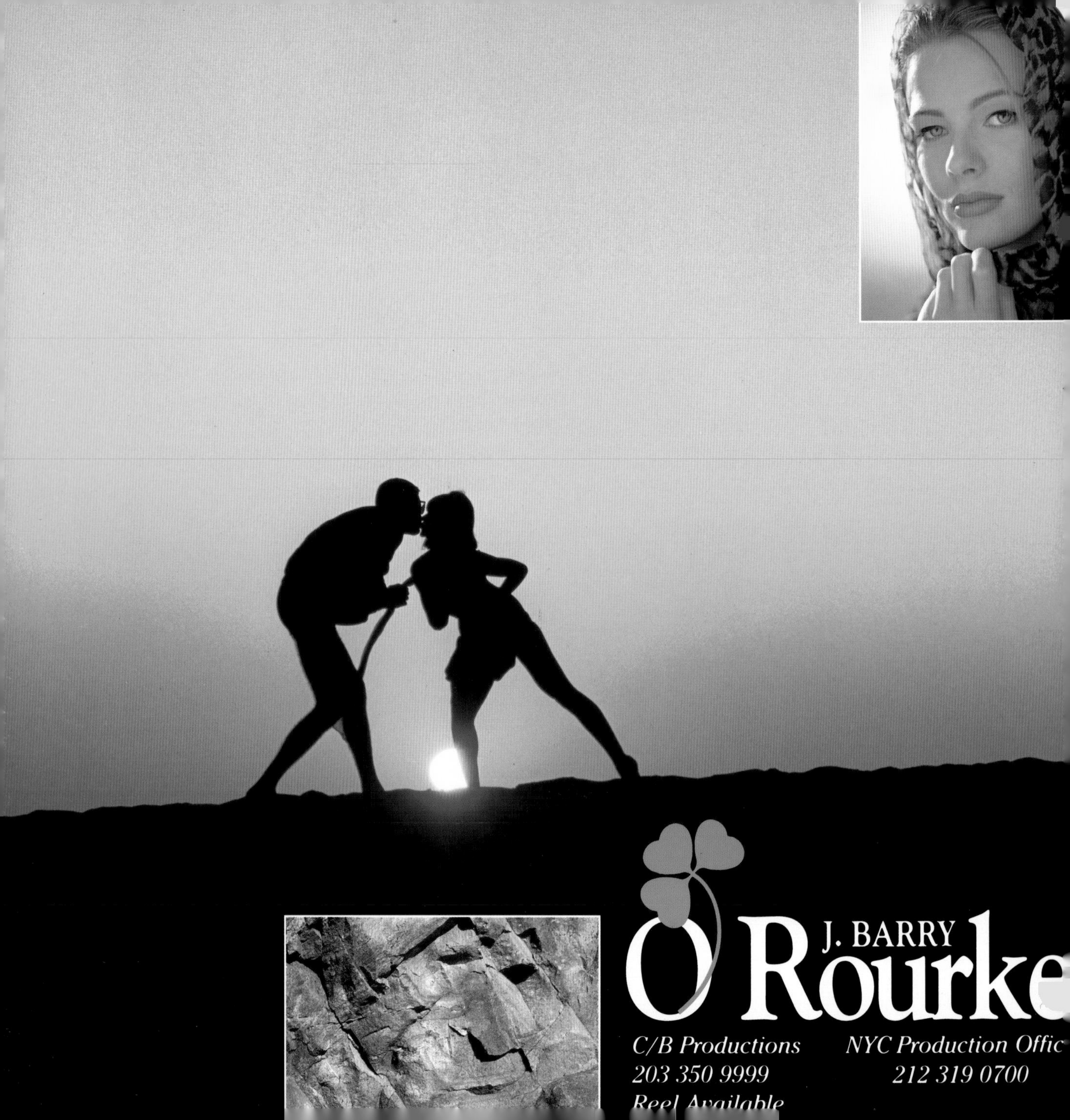

J. BARRY
O'Rourke
C/B Productions
203 350 9999
Reel Available
NYC Production Offic
212 319 0700

Anne Akiko Meyers - RCA Records

James Galway - RCA Records

Harolyn Blackwell - RCA Records

Kyoko Takezawa - RCA Records

R. Greenberg/ S. Ross
Creativity Magazine

H A R R I S

W E L L E S

P H O T O S

2 1 2 . 2 3 3 . 6 6 5 5

Donny Deutsch - Creativity Magazine

L U K E

Larry "Ratso" Sloman author, collaborator on Howard Stern's "Private Parts"

Alger Hiss, Patriot

More Private Parts

594 BROADWAY
SUITE 1106
NEW YORK, N.Y. 10012
TEL: (212) 925-4501
FAX: (212) 925-4718

L O I S

Saville

Lynn Savil

440 Riverside Drive #

New York, NY 100

(212) 932-18

Mark Winston Griffith ▪ Executive Director Central Brooklyn Partnership

Alice Young ▪ Partner Kaye, Scholer

Andre Harrell ▪ President Uptown Entertainment

Roxanne Martinez ▪ Rap Artist

Sherrie Nickol

212 . 666 . 3118

REPRESENTED BY DOROTHEA SCHER 212 689 7273

Sherrie Nickol

212.666.3118

Staff ▪ Punsch Restaurant

Ian Schrager ▪ Royalton Hotel ▪ CEO Morgans Hotel Group

Betsey Johnson ▪ Fashion Designer

Larry Colin ▪ President Colin Service Systems

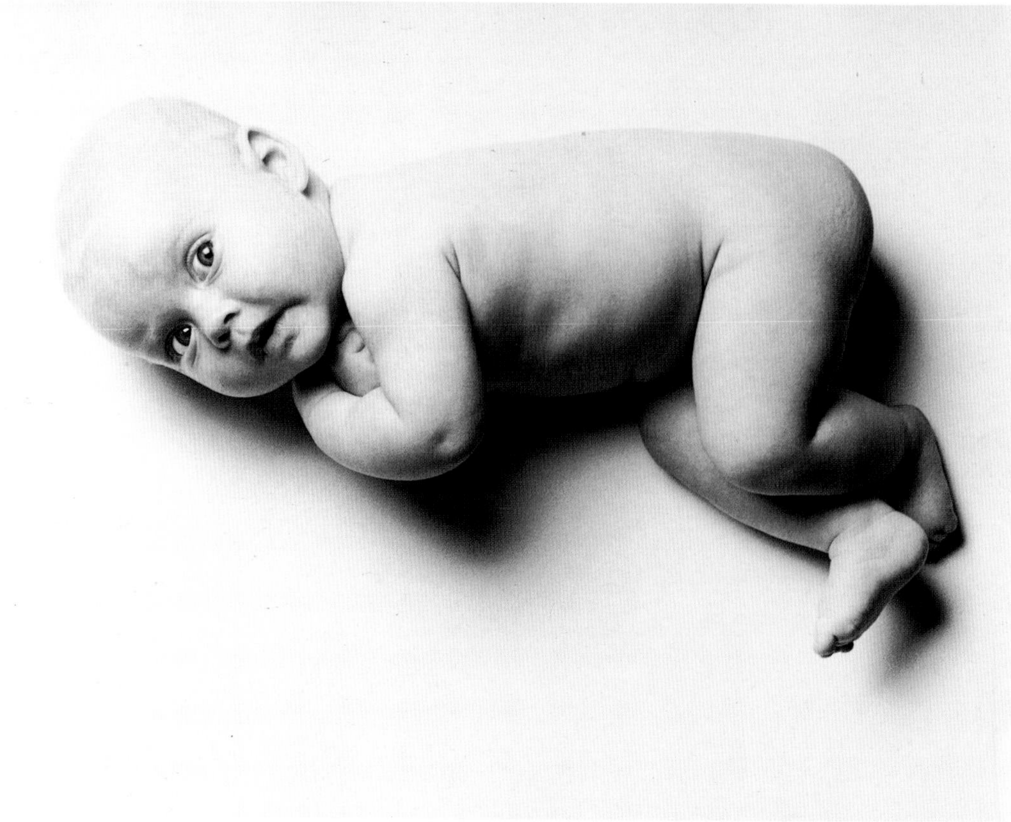

SKALSKI

KEN SKALSKI · PHOTOGRAPHY 873 BROADWAY N.Y. N.Y. 10003 212·777·6207

D E N N I S   M I L B A U E R

126 ELEVENTH AVENUE NEW YORK CITY 10011   212 255 8998

I told the actress I envisioned her looking like the kind of woman you might see standing in front of a trailer home somewhere on the outskirts of Waco, Texas.

When she expressed a lack of enthusiasm for the concept, I told her that we see her standing there by the trailer home just moments before being discovered by a passing Hollywood producer.

I asked the actor to play the part of a simple man about to lose his wife and child to the lure of Celebrity.

BARD MARTIN 212.929.6712

STYLIST CYNTHIA NASH

STYLIST CYNTHIA NASH

Spain was the location,
but there was no money
in the budget for
getting us there.

What to do?

We re-created Spain in
my studio, out of our
memories of the balconies
and flowers and warm
evening light of Seville.

JIM GALANTE STUDIO
STUDIO: 212·529·4300 FAX: 212·529·4332

JIM GALANTE STUDIO

STUDIO: 212•529•4300   FAX: 212•529•4332

MARESCA

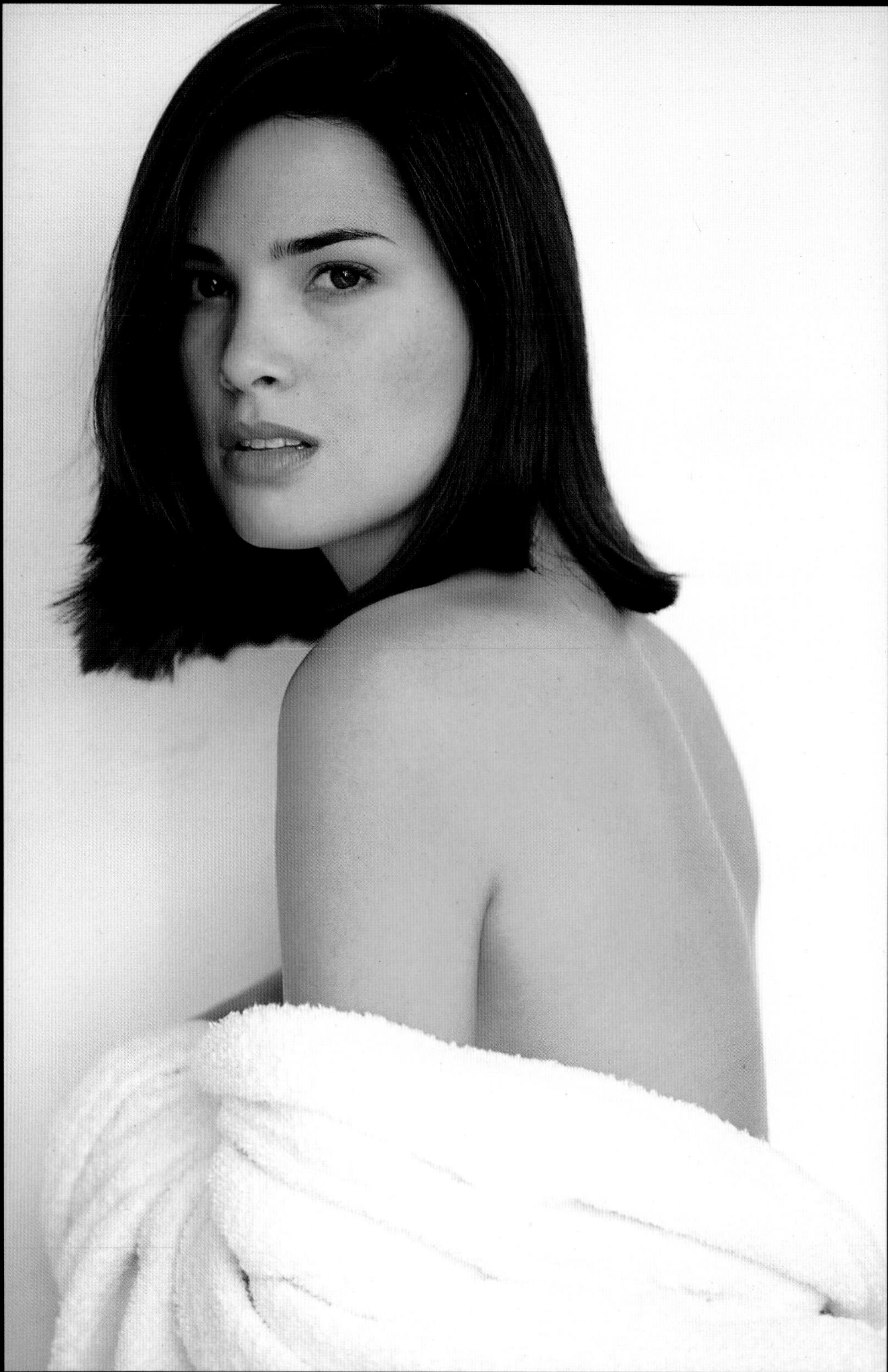

236 W. 26th Street New York, N.Y. 10001 212·620·0955 Fax·620·0961

Caress®
The body bar with bath oil.
Leaves skin feeling
softer than soap can.
Before you dress...Caress.
Caress
Caress

©NANCY BROWN

NANCY BROWN

6 W. 20 ST. NEW YORK, NY 10011 212 924-9105 212 633-0911 FAX

ASMP APA STOCK: IMAGE BANK
STOCK FILM FOOTAGE AND PRINT AVAILABLE

ALLAN LUFTIG

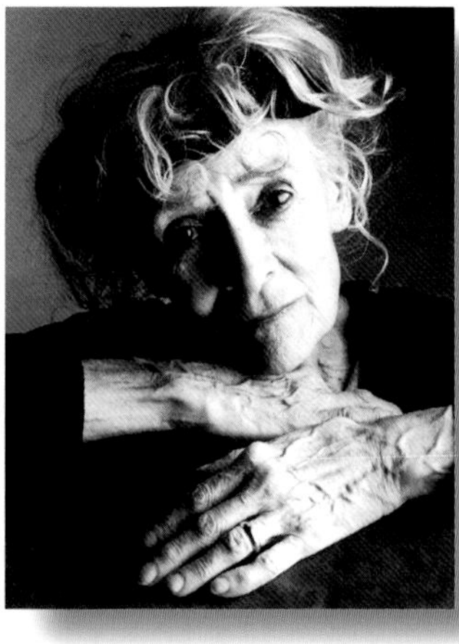

Homework
English - pgs. 12-17

ALLAN LUFTIG STUDIO INC.
873 BROADWAY NEW YORK, NY 10003
TEL 212.533.4113 FAX 212.533.4243

ALLAN LUFTIG

"I want the paint to bring out all the patterns of the various fabrics in my living room. Something that complements both the curtains and the chairs. The mantle and trim should contrast slightly. I'm very particular about color and I know what I want when I see it. Get the colors right and the whole room comes together. Oh, and I want the best paint for the money."
"Got any brilliant ideas?"
A Stroke Of Brilliance.

"I want a paint that can stand up to intense sunlight or anything else the weather dishes out. A paint that keeps its color. The front of my house really takes a beating. So I want a paint that's going to give me the best durability. On top of that, there's a really serious moisture problem. So, I need a paint dealer who can answer some tough questions."
"Got any brilliant ideas?"
A Stroke Of Brilliance.

"I need a paint for wood and masonry that's really going to last and look great on both. And I want a selection of colors which will truly capture the personality of the house and match the flowers in the garden out front. With the trim and eaves I want just enough contrast to help them complement each other."
"Got any brilliant ideas?"
A Stroke Of Brilliance.

LLAN LUFTIG STUDIO INC.
73 BROADWAY NEW YORK, NY 10003
EL 212.533.4113 FAX 212.533.4243

DENNY TILLMAN

212.255.2977

LODGE.
HOTEL

DENNY TILLMAN
212.255.2977

GAS
BAIT & TACKLE
BEER & FOOD
GUARDIAN

hilden * hahn studios

represented in new york by samantha lewin (212) 228 * 5530 * in atlanta by david marriott (404) 303 *

RICHARD LEE

212 989 4502

nyc

NAOKI OKAMOTO NEW YORK 212-864-2447

JIM SULLEY
PHOTOGRAPHER

62 WEST 45TH STREET
NEW YORK NY 10036
(212) 730-8857

ALUMINUM

McGIRT
WHITAKER

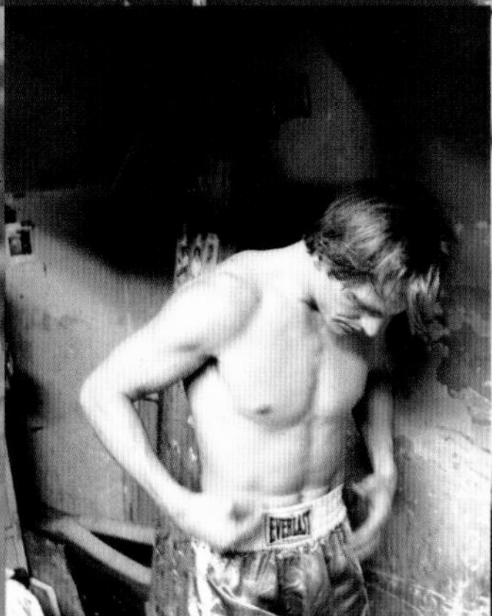
EVERLAST

EVERLAST

EVERLAST

SUGAR RAY ROBINSON

EVERLAST

EVERLAST

07

C.C.B.

HAPPY EASTER!

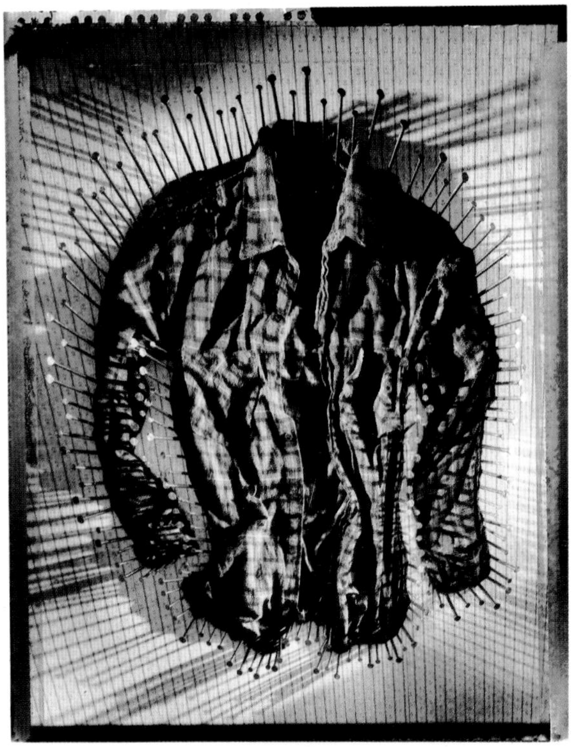

robert lewis 333 park ave south new york city 10010 212·475·6564

IBM
IBM

MATTHEW KLEIN

Studio: 212 255-6400, fax: 212 242-6
Represented by LEVIN•DORR, 212 627-9

MATTHEW KLEIN

Studio: 212 255-6400, fax: 212 242-6149

Represented by LEVIN•DORR, 212 627-9871

William Whitehurst
256 Fifth Ave. New York, NY 10001
212 481 8481

HOUGHTON MIFFLIN

BEAR STEARNS

SMITH BARNEY SHEARSON
FORTUNE
THE FORTUNE 500
THE LARGEST U.S. INDUSTRIAL CORPORATIONS
HOW THEY RANK BY SALES, PROFITS, INVESTMENT PERFORMANCE, AND MANY OTHER MEASURES
GRAND HOTEL DE PEKIN
HOTEL COLOMBIA
William Whitehurst
256 Fifth Ave. NewYork, NY 10001
212 481 8481

SUSANNE BUCKLER

348 West 38th Street
New York, NY 10018
tel: 212.279.0043
tel: 203.866.8845

NY Times Magazine

Tiffany & Co

Asprey, New York

KENRO IZU

140 West 22nd Street, New York, N.Y. 10011, (212) 254-1002
REPRESENTED BY JEAN CONLON (212) 966-9897

DeSANTO
THOM DESANTO PHOTOGRAPHY INC. 116 WEST 29 STREET NEW YORK, NEW YORK 10001 212.967.1390
AGENT/ KEVIN R. SCHOCHAT 212.475.7068 FACSIMILE 212.475.1040

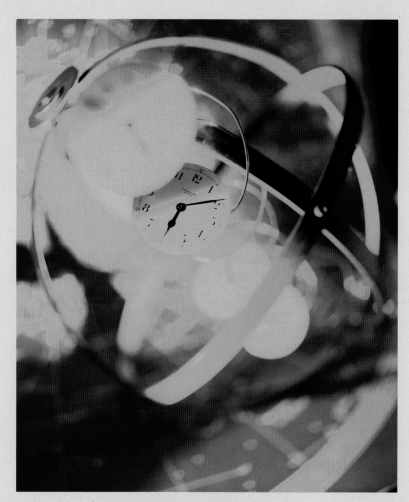

JOHN WILKES STUDIO

Robert TARDIO

REPRESENTED BY COLLEEN MCKAY
TELEPHONE 212 598 0469

STUDIO TELEPHONE 212 254 5413

Dylan Cross

Represented by Stephanie Thomas 212 727 1977

ANNICK GOUTAL
Eau d'Hadrien
PARIS

MARTELL
MARTELL

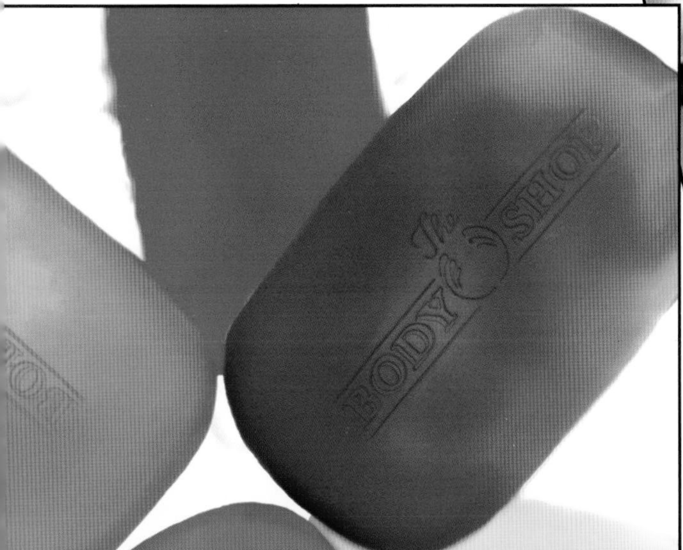
The BODY SHOP
The BODY SHOP

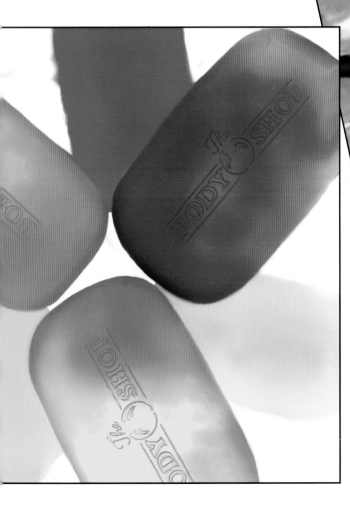

Susan Goldman New York 212 255 4564

Susan Goldman New York 212 255 4564

CORN
SWEET CORN
SWEET CORN
SWEET CORN

37 West 20th St. New York, NY 10011 212.727.3884

Steve Cohen

Represented by Elka Kristo-Nagy 212.255.752

SURFACES

West 20th St. New York, NY 10011 212.727.3884

Steve Cohen

Represented by Elka Kristo-Nagy 212.255.7525

Club

CHARLES MARAIA

236 West 27th Street No.804 New York NY 10001 212.206.8156

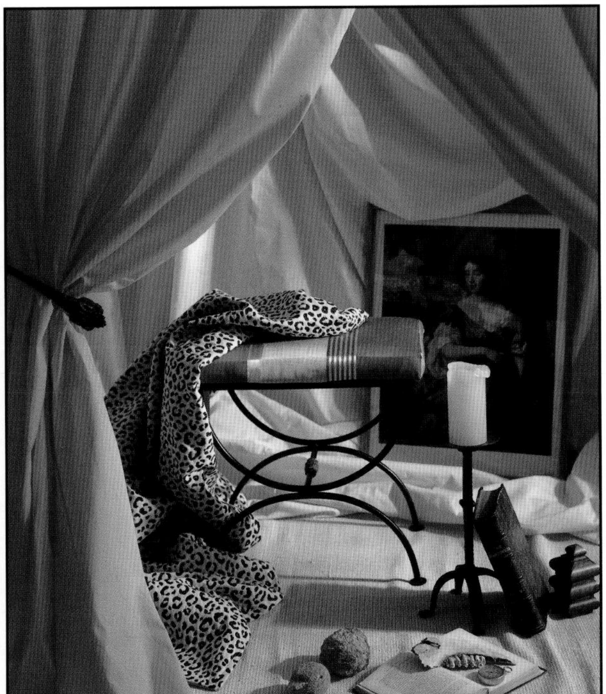

Cabotine
de
GRÈS

RICKY NG
photography

KATHY BRUML
212 874-5659
Agent

RICKY NG

photography

KATHY BRUML

212 874-5659

Agent

HELLERSTEIN.

sixfourfivezerofivezeroeight[newyorkcity]

PHOTOGRAMS
ILLUSTRATE

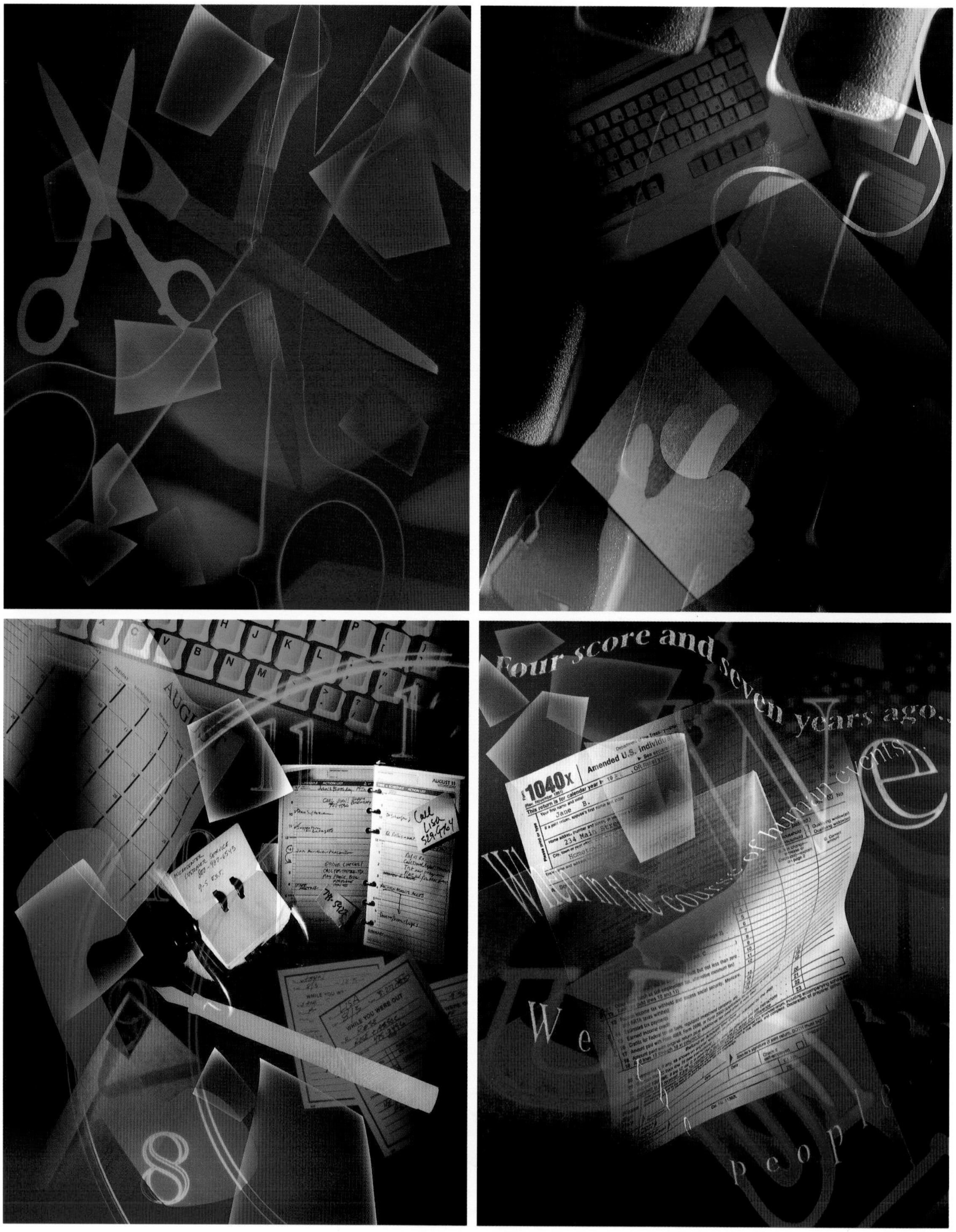
AUGUST
WHILE YOU WERE OUT
Four score and seven years ago..
1040X
Amended U.S. Individual
When in the course of human events
We the people

BILL WESTHEIMER

167-169 Spring Street
New York, New York 10012
☎ [212] 431•6360 Fax: [212] 431•5496

LUMIÈRE

BART GORIN

126 ELEVENTH AVE., NYC 10011 (212) 727-7344

BART GORIN

126 ELEVENTH AVE., NYC 10011 (212) 727-7344

RIC COHN NYC 212 924 4450 REPRESENTED BY CAROL COHN

He didn't
believe in bad luck,

of course,

he didn't believe in
good luck
either.

But the deal came through -
and Jules was on top
of the world.

Basking
in this triumph,
he thought,
could only be
better with
her.

(meet her in the '95 Black Book)

RIC COHN
212 924 4450

Westclo

Dennis Galante new york city 212 529-5531

109.84
2.7775
1.786
3.7752
1.6155
3.5746

Represented by Samantha Lewin 212 228-5530

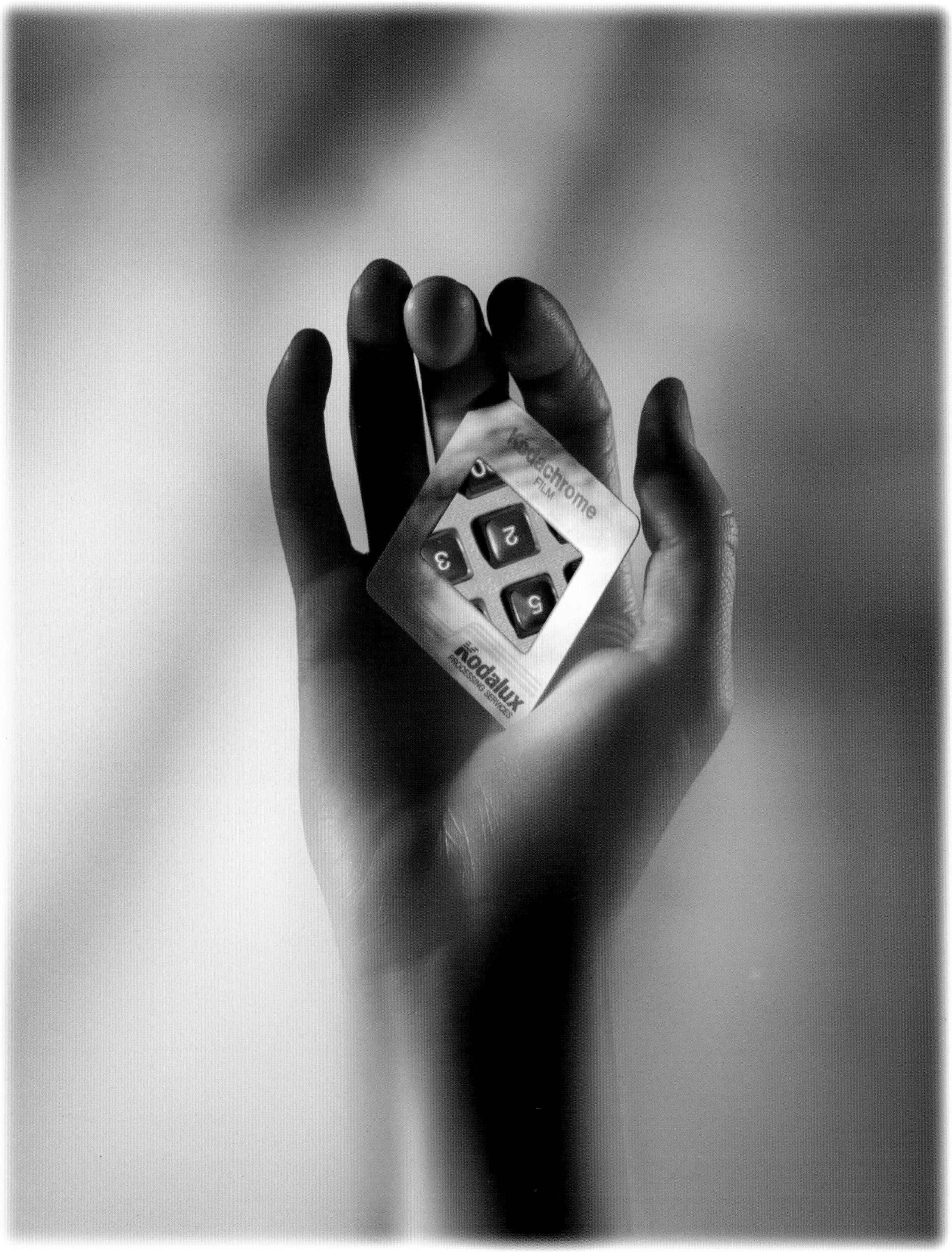
Kodachrome
FILM
Kodalux
PROCESSING SERVICES
3
2
5

Dennis Galante new york city 212 529-5531

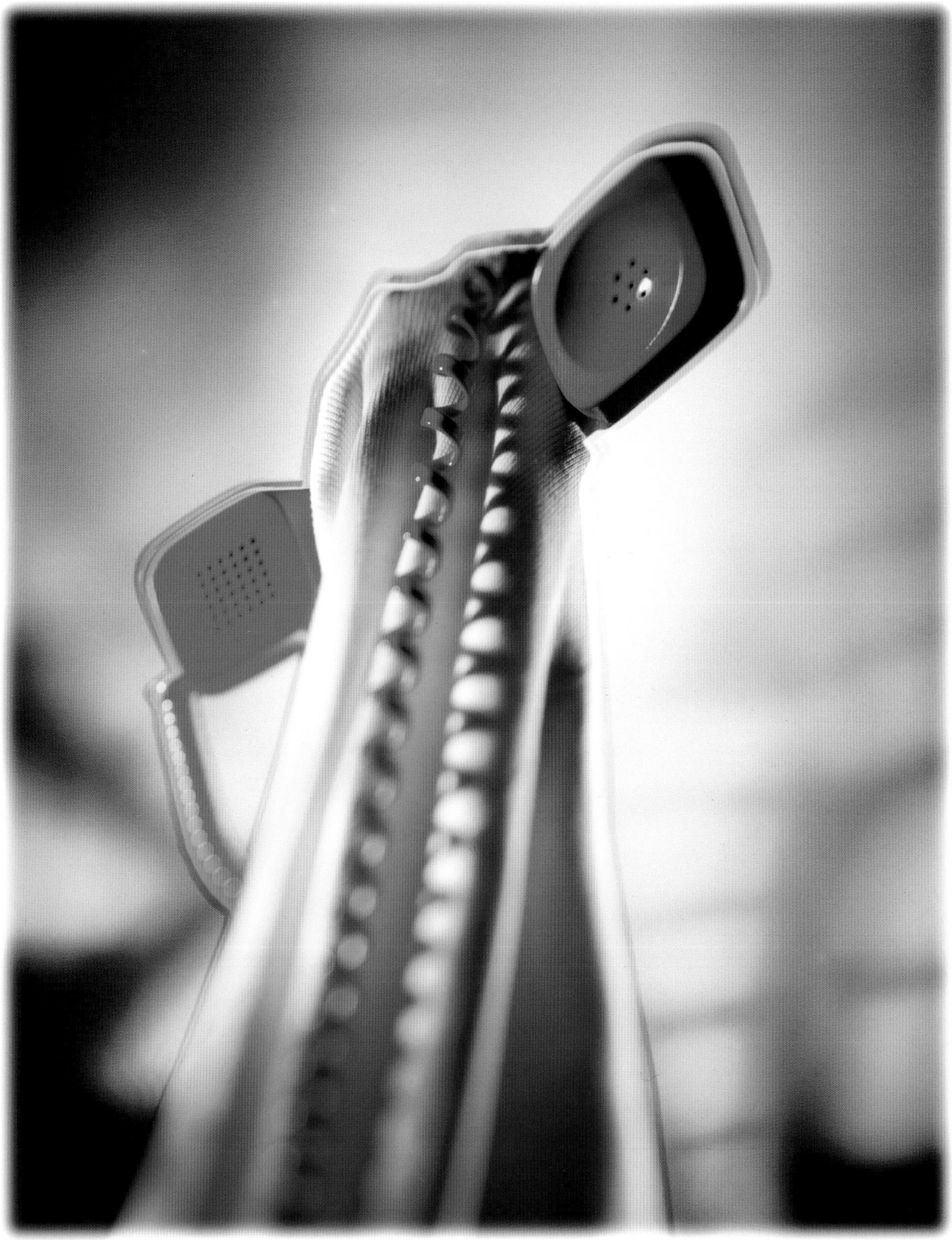

Represented by Samantha Lewin 212 228-5530

kosoff

Brian Kosoff
28 West 25 Street
New York, NY 10010
212 243 4880
Fax 212 727 2044

kosoff

Brian Kosoff
28 West 25 Street
New York, NY 10010

212 243 4880
Fax 212 727 2044

HOT

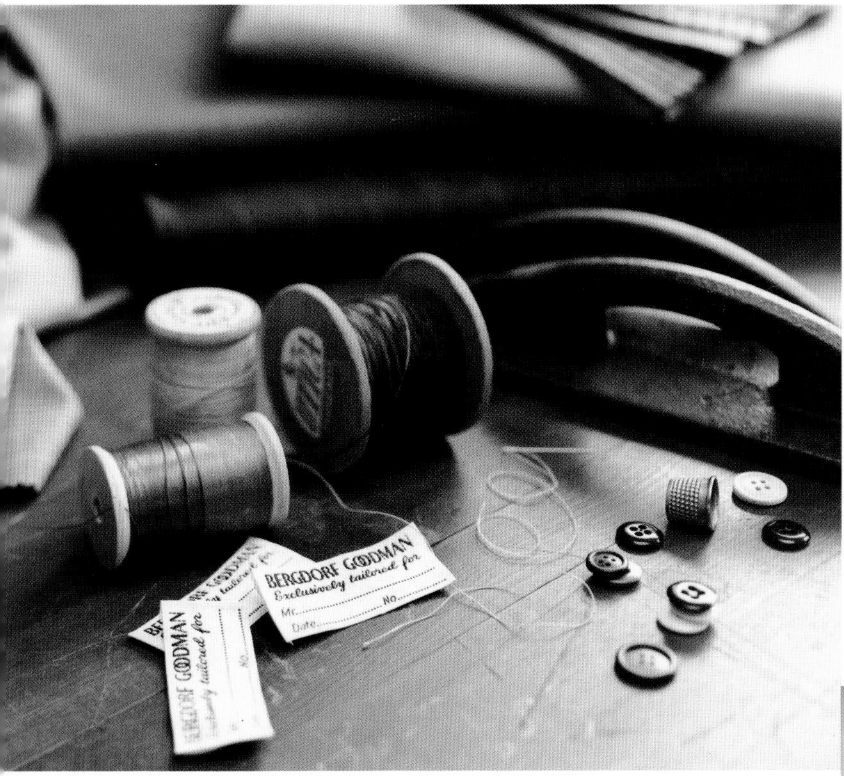
BERGDORF GOODMAN
Exclusively tailored for
Mr. No.
Date

douglas rosa photography
122 west 26th street
new york city, ny 10001

rosa

212 366 4898
fax 212 924 2760

Rick Osentoski

Tel. – 212 679 5919

ESTĒE LAUDER
DEMI-MATTE
LIQUID MAKEUP
Fond de teint fluide

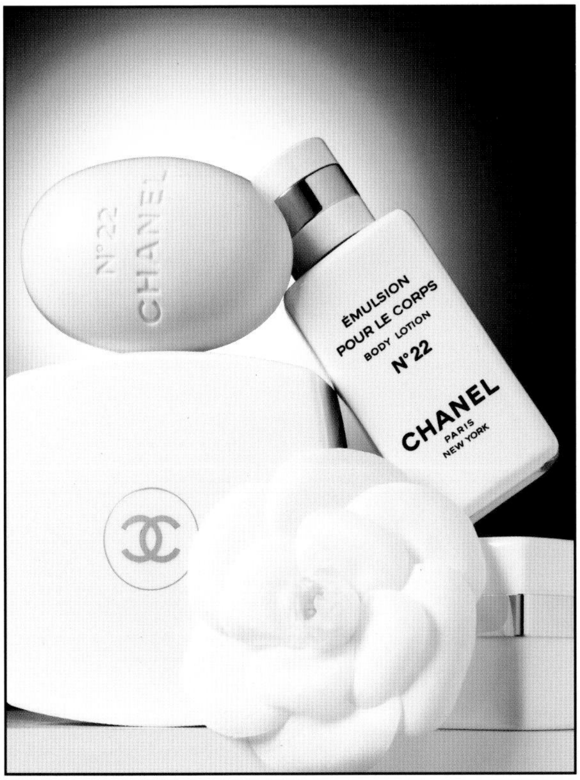
N°22
CHANEL
ÉMULSION
POUR LE CORPS
BODY LOTION
N°22
CHANEL
PARIS
NEW YORK

VAPORISATEUR
EAU DE TOILETTE
NATURAL SPRAY

9601 ENRIQUE CUBILLO 212 243 9601 ENRIQUE CUBILLO 212 243 9601 ENR

CUBILLO 212 243 9601 ENRIQUE CUBILLO 212 243 9601 ENRIQUE CUBILLO 21

HB
2
HB

LLO 212 243 9601 ENRIQUE CUBILLO 212 243 9601 ENRIQUE CUBILLO 212 24

1 ENRIQUE CUBILLO 212 243 9601 ENRIQUE CUBILLO 212 243 9601 ENRIQUE

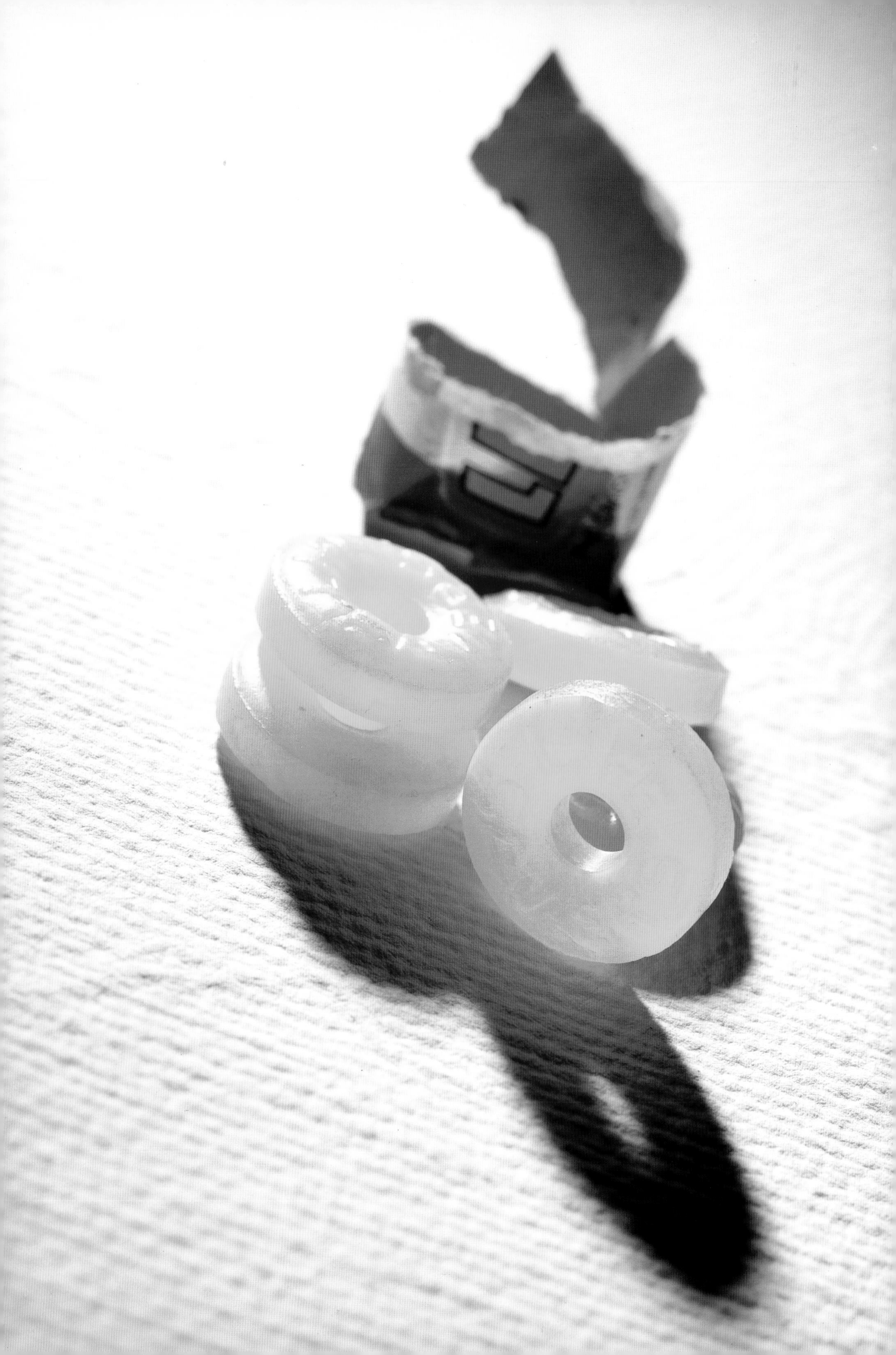

SIMON METZ PHOTOGRAPHY

56 WEST 22ND STREET NEW YORK NY 10010
TEL 212.807.6106 FAX 212.929.8716
REPRESENTED BY JOHN HENRY 212.686.6883

Christian Dior

JOHN PARNELL

16 WAVERLY PLACE

NEW YORK, NY 10003

212 979-9550

PARNELL

"I Love You"
American Sign La
KR-64

P A R N E L L

JOHN PARNELL
16 WAVERLY PLACE
NEW YORK, NY 10003
212 979-9550

tullis

Marcus Tullis is associated with **LIGHT + FORM INC**
Studio:13-17 Laight Street N.Y.C. 1001
212-966-8511 ♦ fax 212-219-14

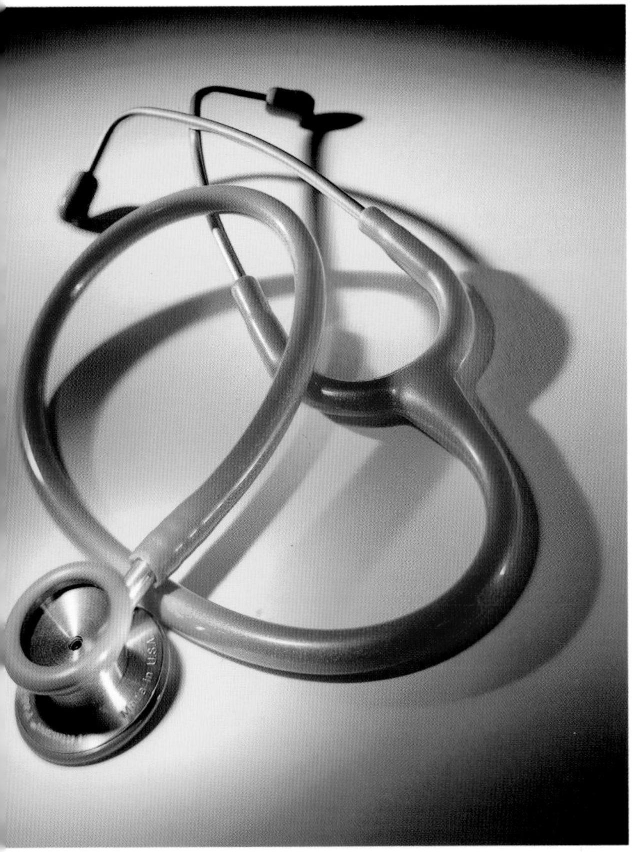

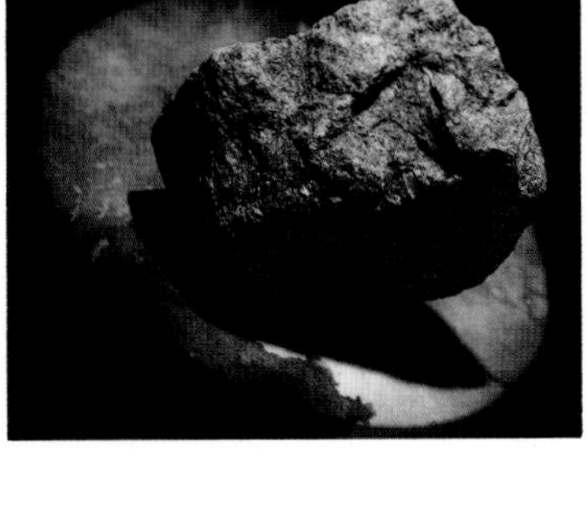

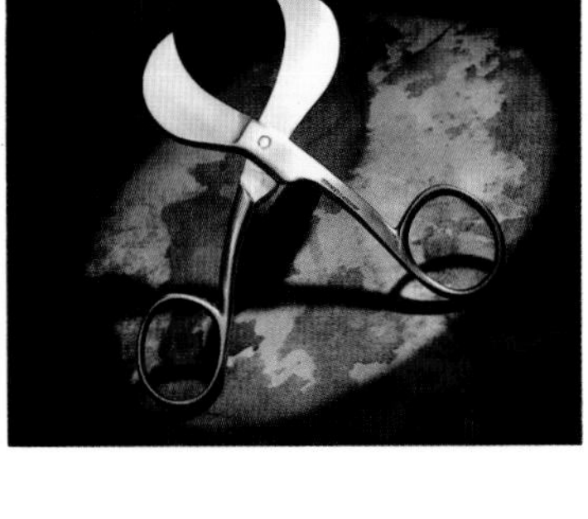

Nicholas Eveleigh

121 Madison Avenue, New York. 212-685-0577

david Sacks

Red
Circle
Studi
5
West
19th
Stree
5TH
floor
New
York
City
1001

212.924.1345

212.675.5540 FAX

Joe Standart
Red Circle Studio
5 West 19th Street
New York City 10011
212 924-4545
212 675-5540 fax
Reel Available

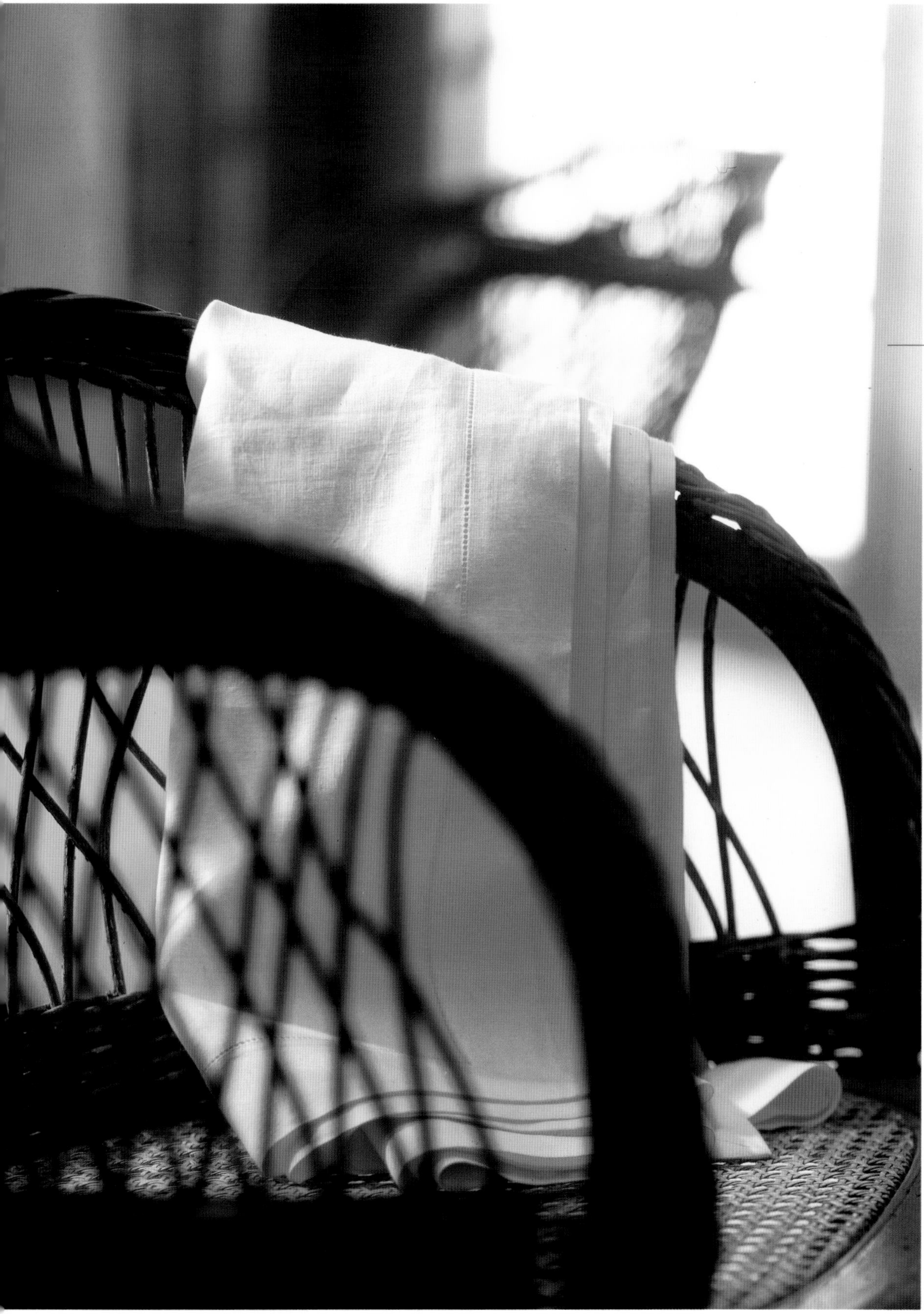

Joe Standart
Red Circle Studio
5 West 19th Street
New York City 10011
212 924-4545
212 675-5540 fax
Reel Available

CITIZEN
FOSSIL
SEIKO
QUARTZ
Chronograph
SPORTS 150
SWISS ARMY
swatch
SWISS

ERIC
HUANG
TEL 212
260 2147

MOSSIMO

ERIC
HUANG
TEL 212
260 2147

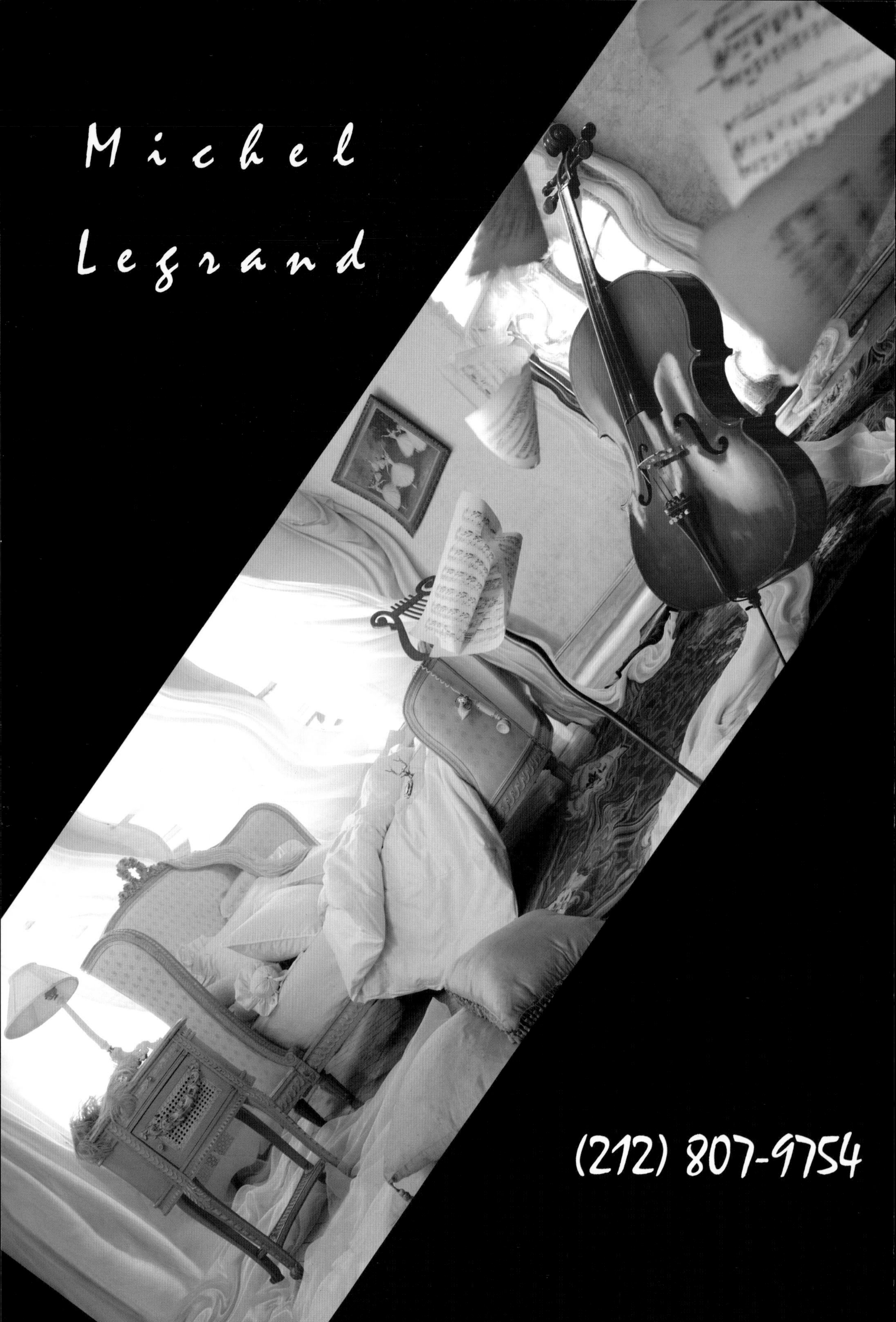

Buon...Appetito!

Photo from BON APPETIT Magazine May 1994

MISTRETTA

REPRESENTED BY LIZ LI 212-889-7067 FAX: 212-685-8189

REPRESENTED BY ROBERT BACALL

TELEPHONE 212.254.5725

380 LAFAYETTE STREET • NYC 10003

Colin Cook

REPRESENTED BY ROBERT BACALL

TELEPHONE 212.254.5725

380 LAFAYETTE STREET • NYC 10003

Colin Cook

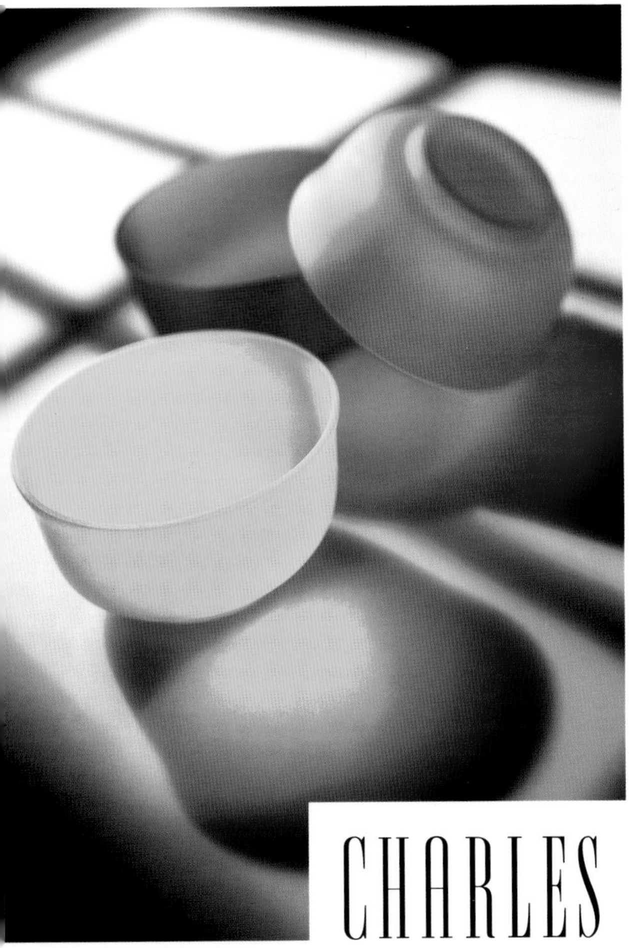

ETERNITY

CHARLES SCHILLER

P H O T O G R A P H Y
2 1 2 . 9 4 1 . 7 6 5 9

CUPS — 16 OZ
CUPS — 12 OZ

LATTUGA
Sapone per pelli delicate

MARY ELLEN BARTLEY
23 Leonard Street 4th floor New York, NY 10013 212 334-9026

Bigger.
Better.
The buttons & handset are bigger.
And that's better for you.
Lease the Big Button Plus
and get the security of AT&T Lease Service.

WHAT MAKES
ICHIBAN
TRULY
DISTINCTIVE?
Imported Ichiban beer is brewed entirely from the "first press" of wort. Other beers use the same wort twice or more and combine the results. Using wort just once makes Ichiban the purest, most flavorful beer in the world.
First-Press
Kirin Ichiban–
The purest beer
in the world.
KIRIN
ICHIBAN
IMPORTED
KIRIN'S PRIME BREW
IMPORTED BEER
KIRIN ICHIBAN
一番搾り

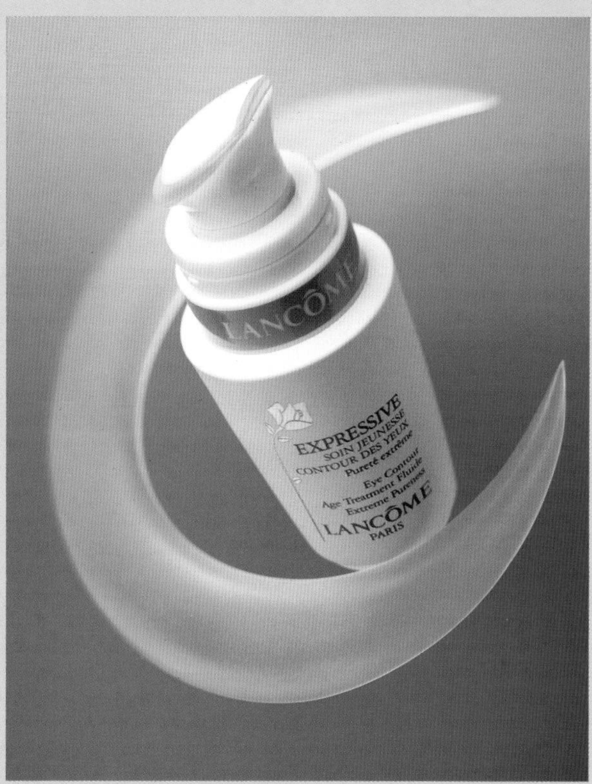

LANCÔME
EXPRESSIVE
SOIN JEUNESSE
CONTOUR DES YEUX
Pureté extrême
Eye Contour
Age Treatment Fluide
Extreme Pureness
LANCÔME
PARIS

PETER ZERAY

113 EAST 12TH STREET NYC 10003 TEL 212 674 0332 FAX 212 674 0755

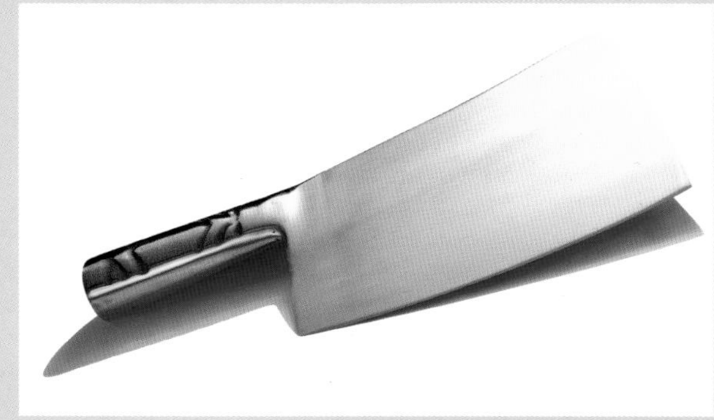

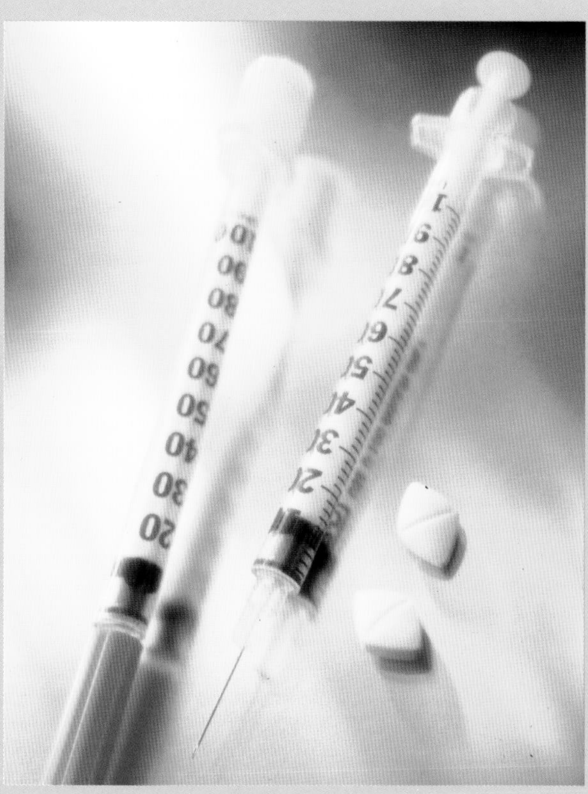

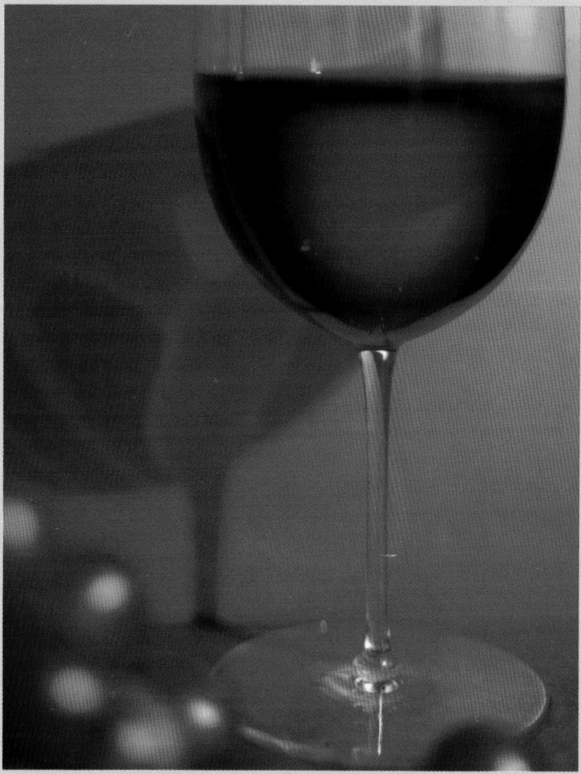

PETER ZERAY

113 EAST 12TH STREET NYC 10003 TEL 212 674 0332 FAX 212 674 0755

NIKE
AIR

AMY REICHMA
PHOTOGRAPHE
212 • 691 • 671

236 W 27 ST • NYC 10001 • FAX 212 • 691 • 6942

(212)929-1078 (212)929-108
PHOTOGRAP
27 W.24TH ST. NEW YORK, NY 10010
STEVE LESNICK

VE LESNICK 27 W. 24TH ST. NEW YORK, NY

Degree
BODY HEAT ACTIVATED

AMERICAN EXPRESS
OPTIMA
AMERICAN EXPRESS

PHOTOGRAPHER
(212)929-1078 (212)929-1084(FAX)

ELIZABETH WATT

PHOTOGRAPHY

141 west 26th street

new york 10001

212 929-8504

fax 212 645-4288

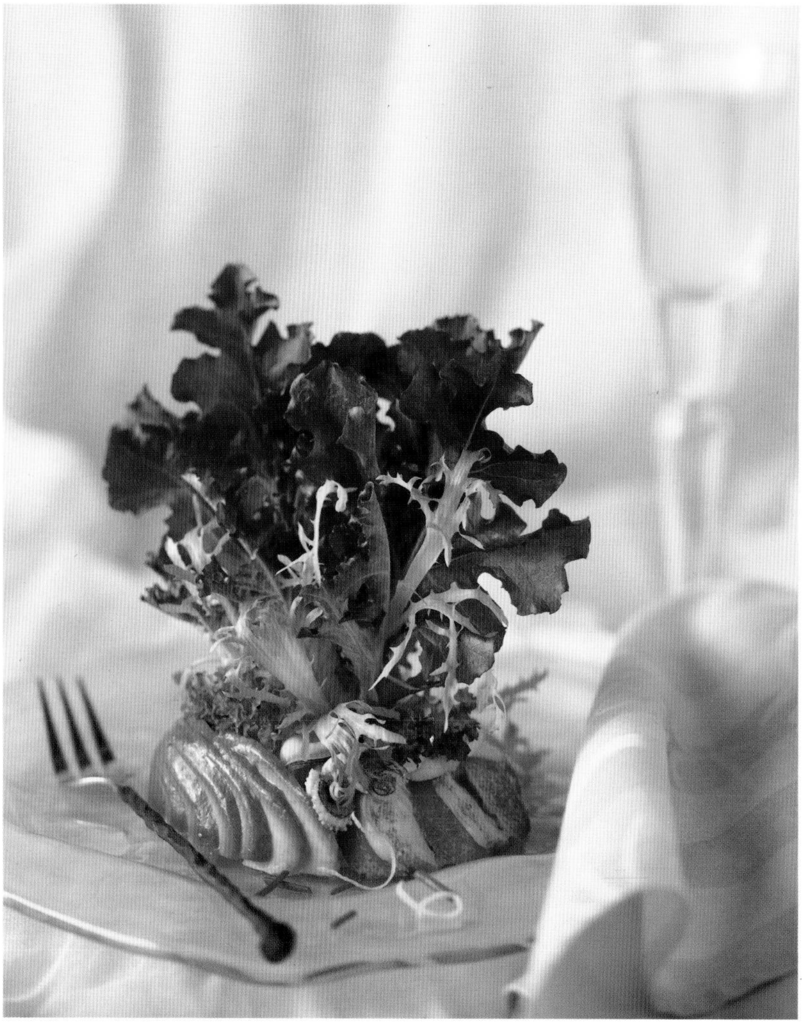

FOOD STYLING BY DORA JONASSEN

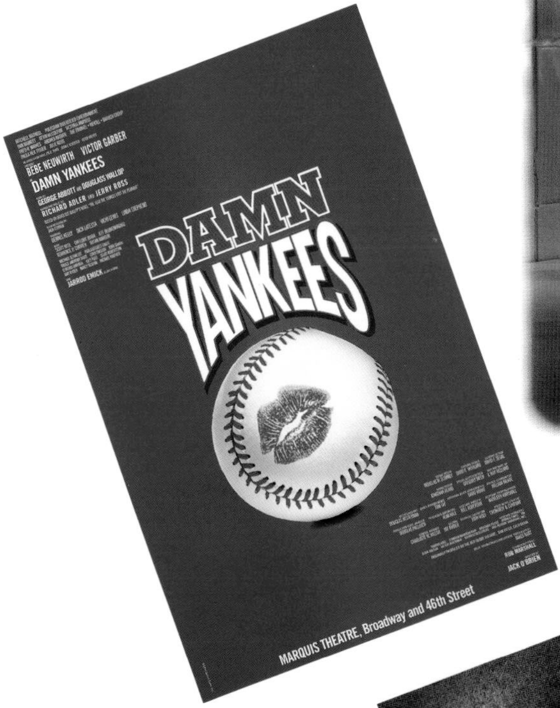
BEBE NEUWIRTH VICTOR GARBER
DAMN YANKEES
GEORGE ABBOTT and DOUGLASS WALLOP
RICHARD ADLER and JERRY ROSS
JARROD EMICK
DAMN YANKEES
ROB MARSHALL
JACK O'BRIEN
MARQUIS THEATRE, Broadway and 46th Street

New!
NIGHT GUARD
OVERNIGHT MOUTHRINSE
Rinse Before Bed
Awaken with Fresher, Cleaner Breath
Plax

Bill Blass
100% CAMEL HAIR

ARTIST
OIL
COLOR

Jon Holderer
37 West 20th Street, NYC
212.620.4260

DAVID HAUTZIG PHOTOGRAPHY

209 East 25th Street • New York, NY 10010
212•779•1595

David also photographs Lifestyle Interiors. Turn to the People section.

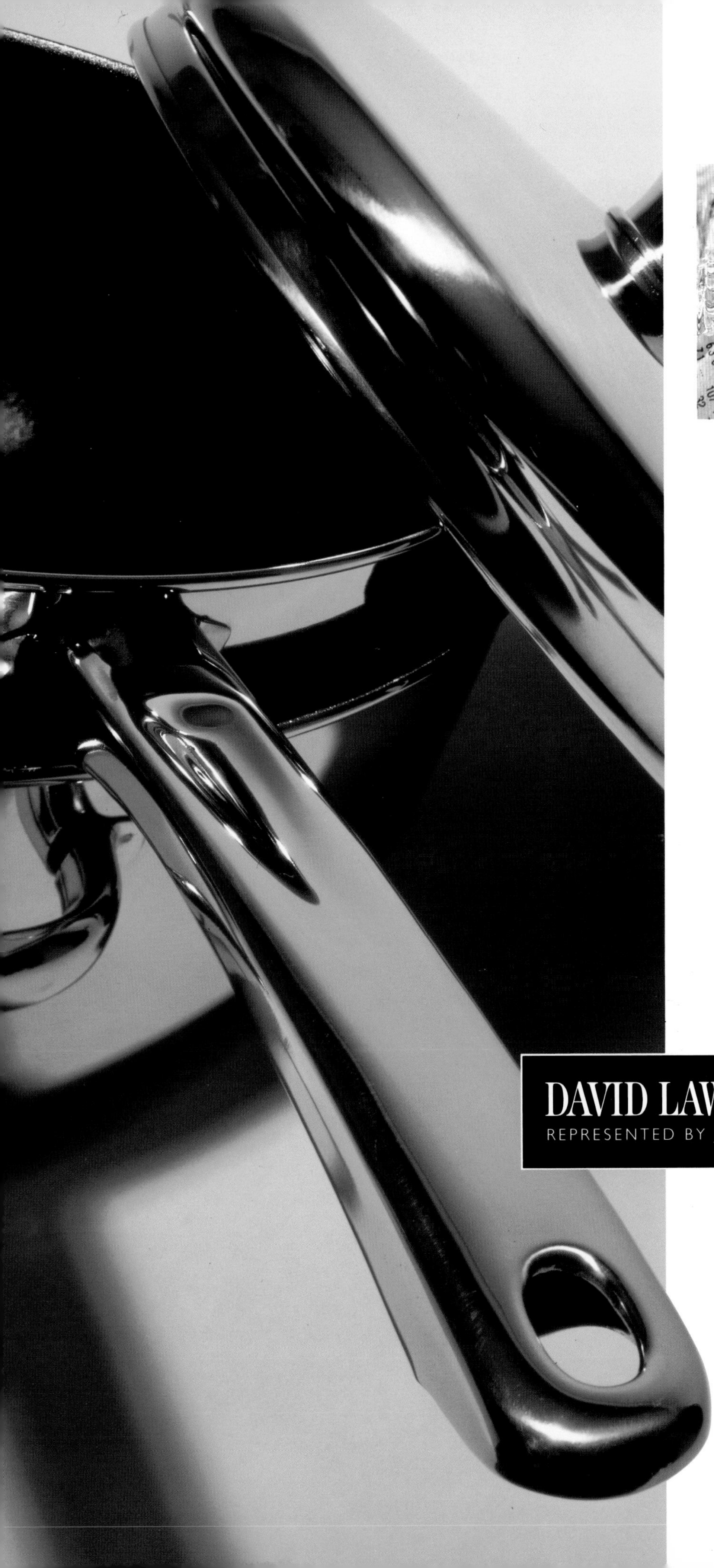

DAVID LAWRENCE *274·0710*

REPRESENTED BY JANICE MOSES 212•779•7929

KODAK / RUMRILL HOYT

BRAD GUICE

212.941.6096

232 WEST BROADWAY NYC 10013

REPRESENTED BY

JANICE MOSES

212.779.7929

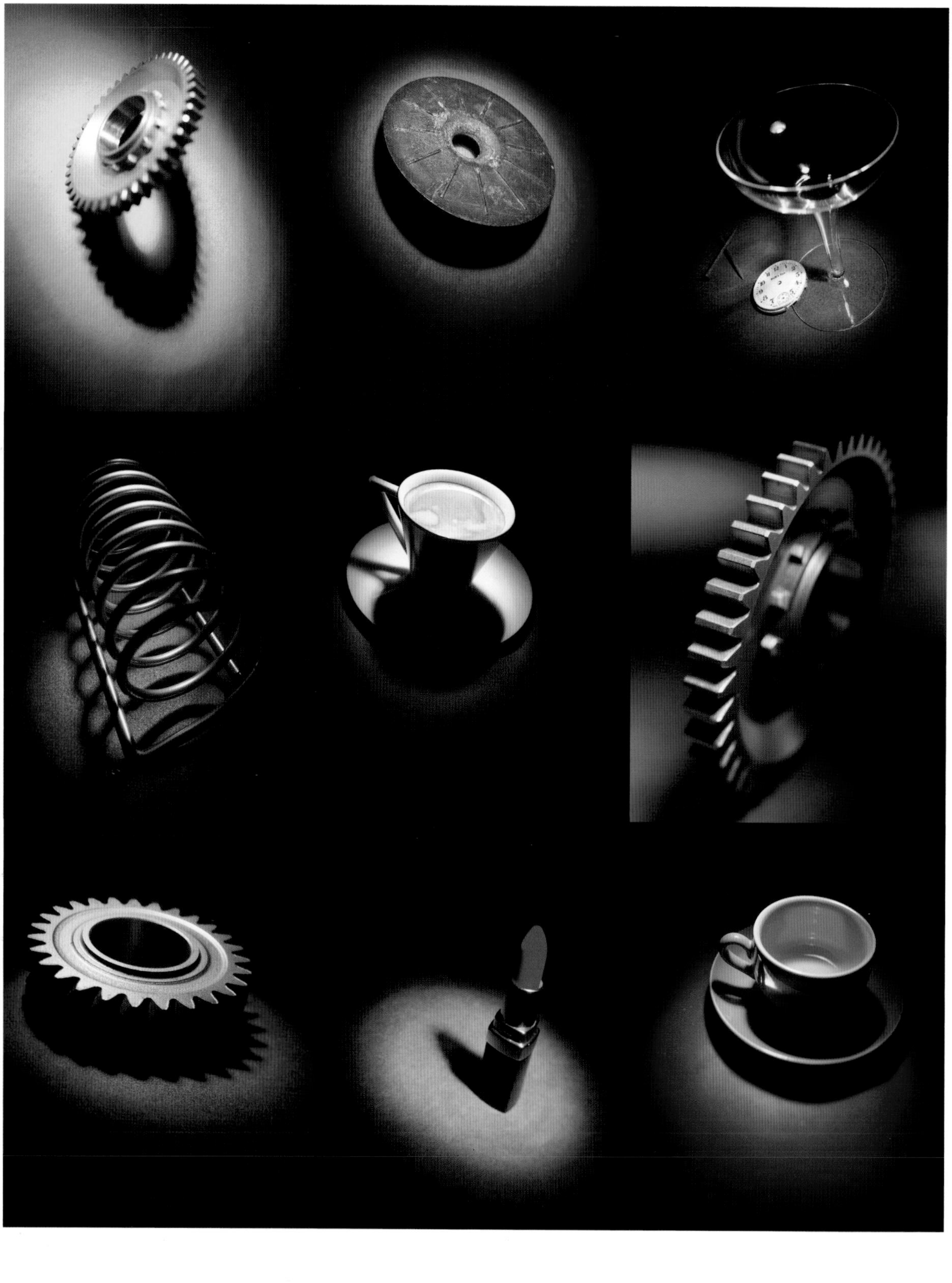

RICHARD GREENE 212.460.5546

alan holstein @ 212·957·8345

Bain
Moussant
à la
Lavande
La Baignoire

the slip

chris
de
gray

PHOTOGRAPHY

119 West 23 Street Suite 601 NYC Studio 212.633.1577 Fax 212.255.9088

CONTACT MARGE CASEY 212.486.9575

NORA SCARLETT

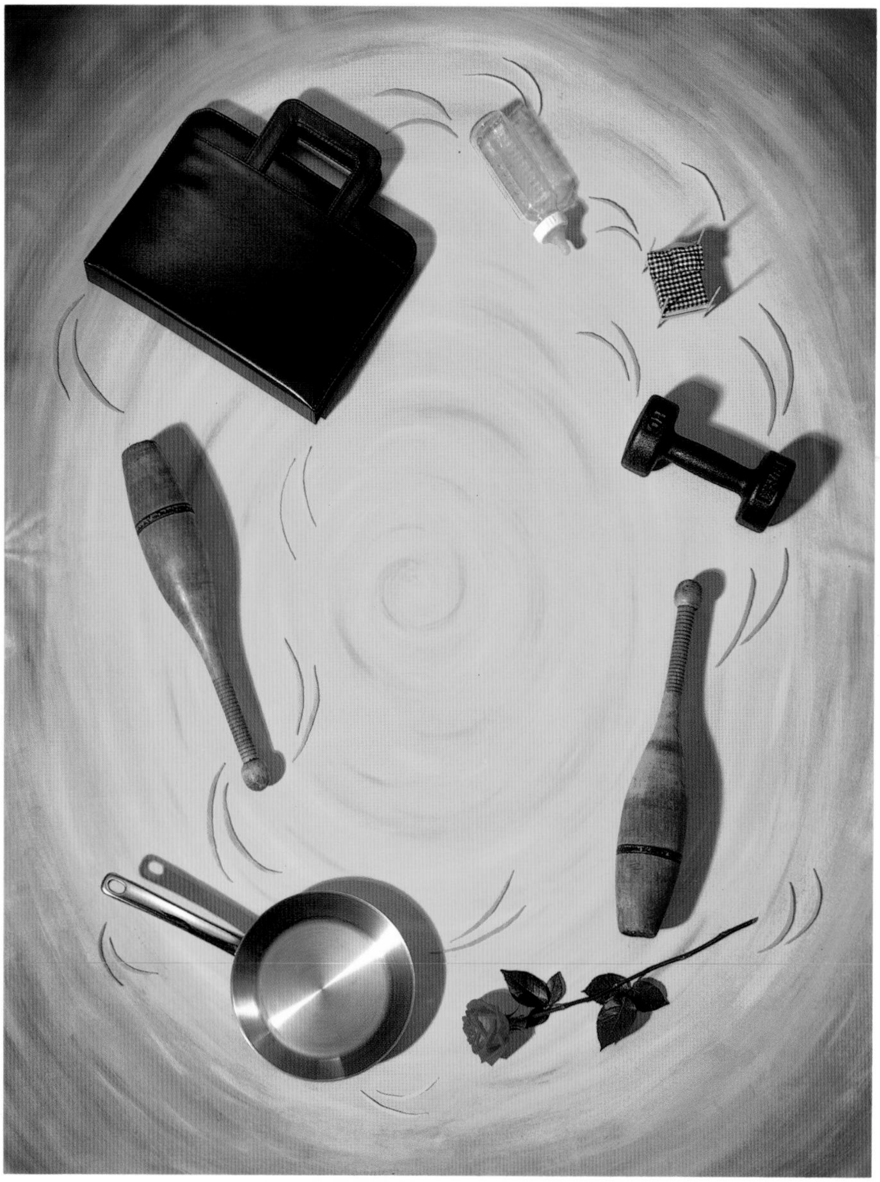

37 WEST 20TH STREET NYC 10011
212 741 2620

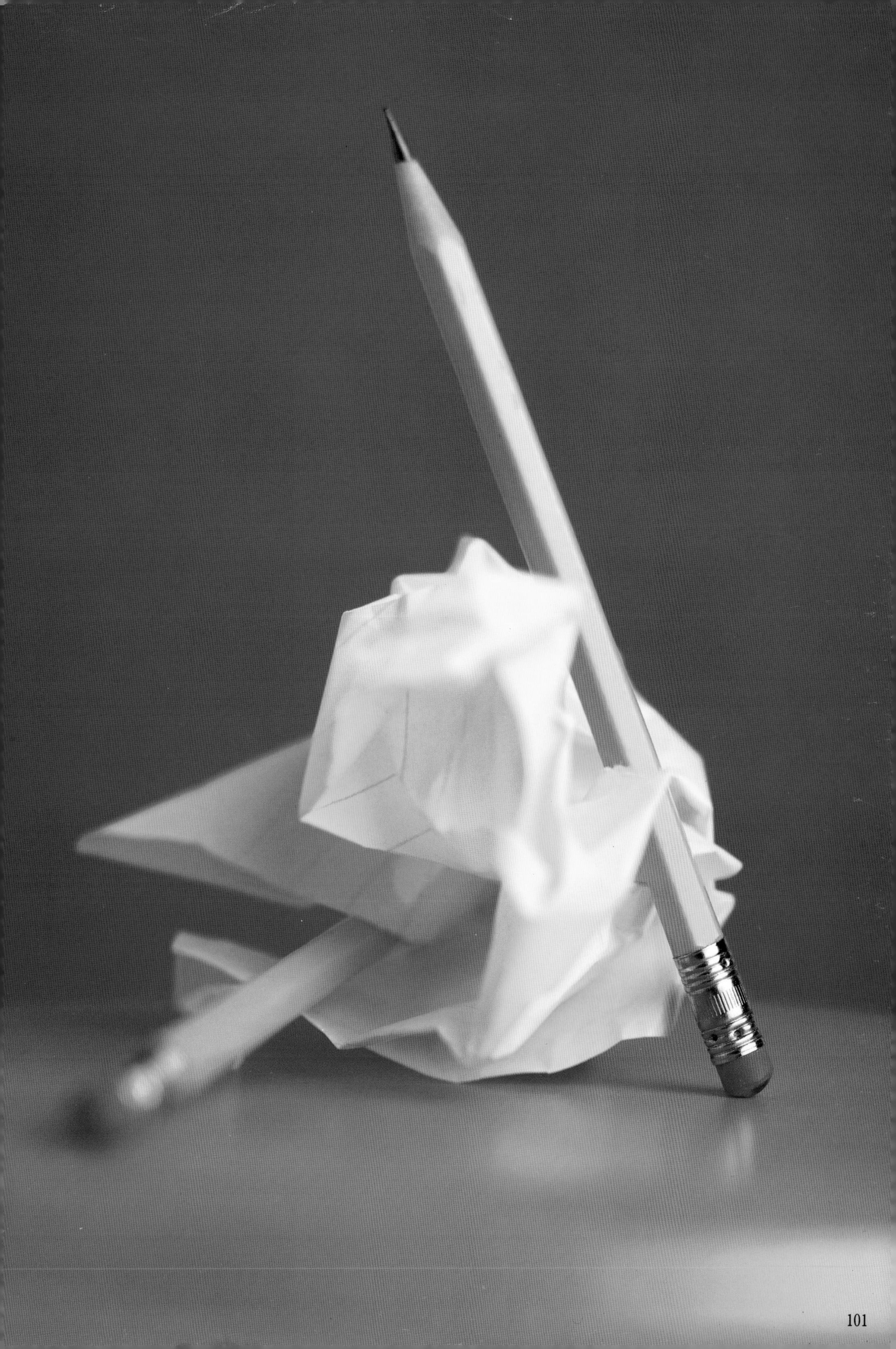

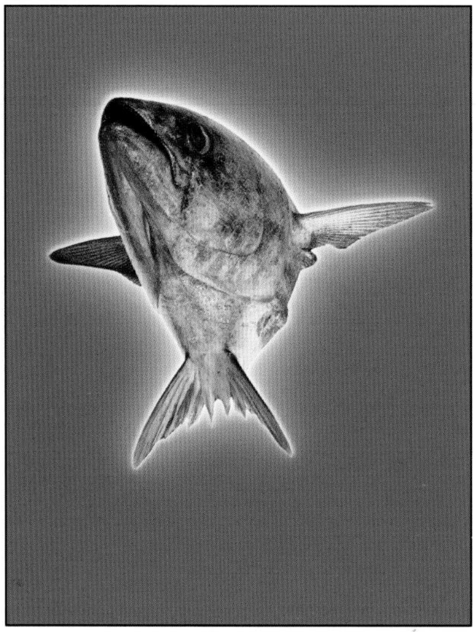

MOOSEHEAD
ICE
Canadian
BEER
12 fl. oz. · 5.6% alc./vol.

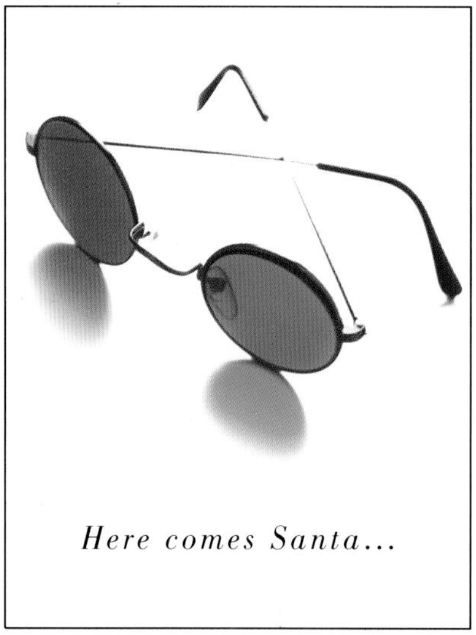
Here comes Santa...

Seaweed
Aroma Art

KRYPELL KRYPELL

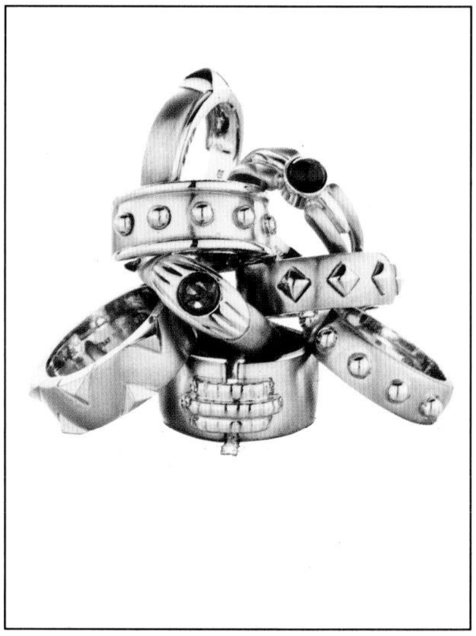

RON SALTIEL
78 FIFTH AVENUE
NEW YORK, NY 10011
(212) 627-0003
(212) 627-1301 FAX

MW

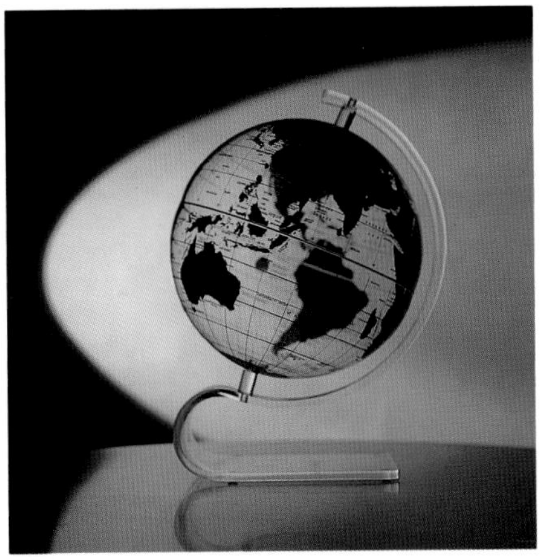

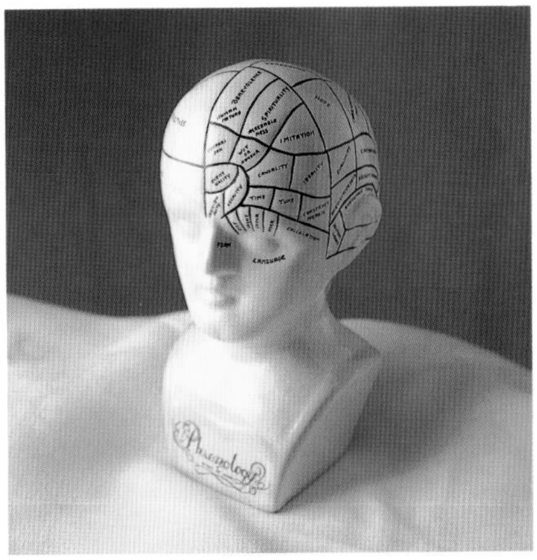

Michael Watson Studio

133 West 19th Street New York, New York 10011 fax: 212-627-3798 phone: 212-620-3125

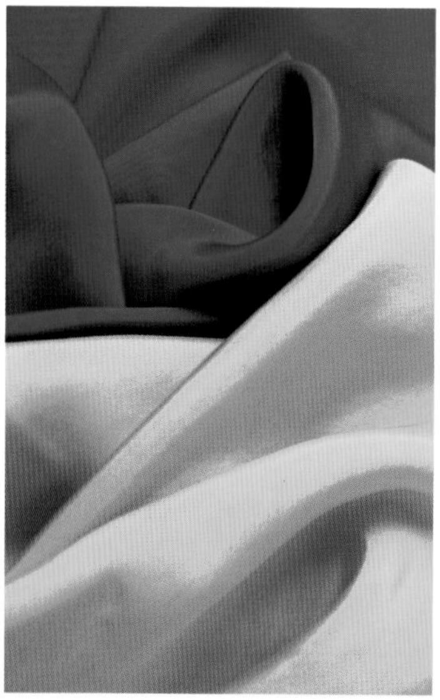

Luigi Cazzaniga
212-228-6690
Fax 212-260-2256

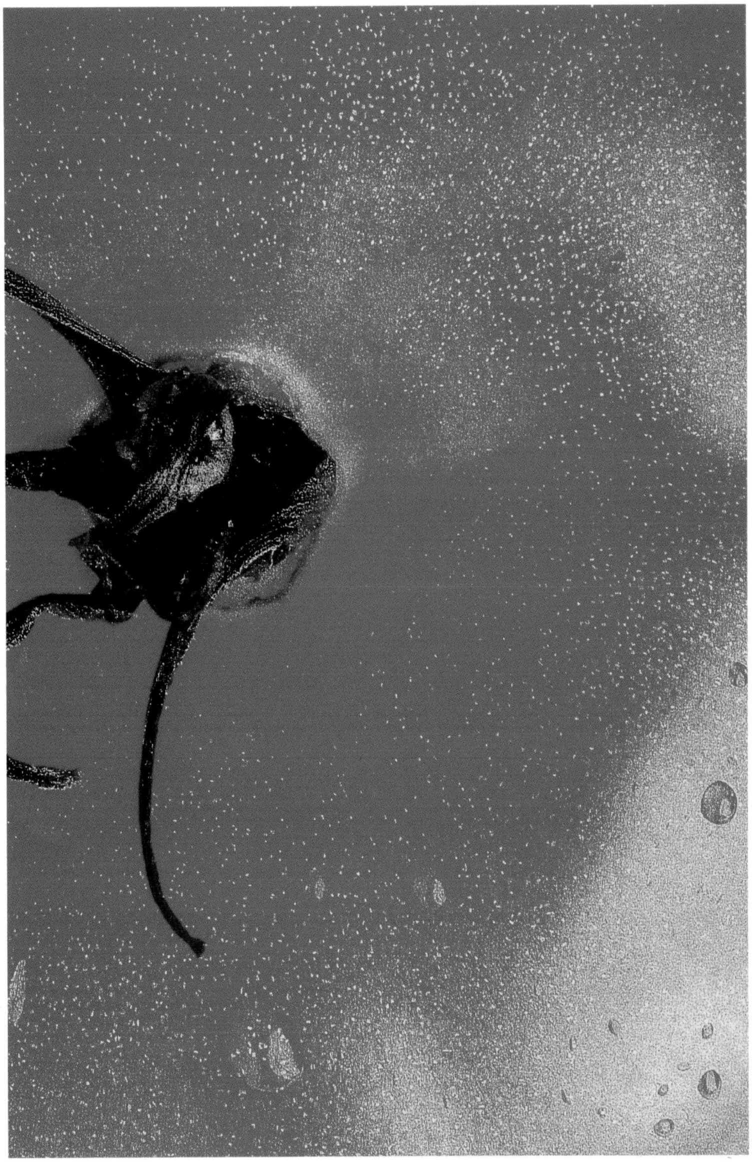

Luigi Cazzaniga
212-228-6690
Fax 212-260-2256

ESTĒE
Moisturizing Body Lotion

NEC
Express RISCserver

TRADITIONAL

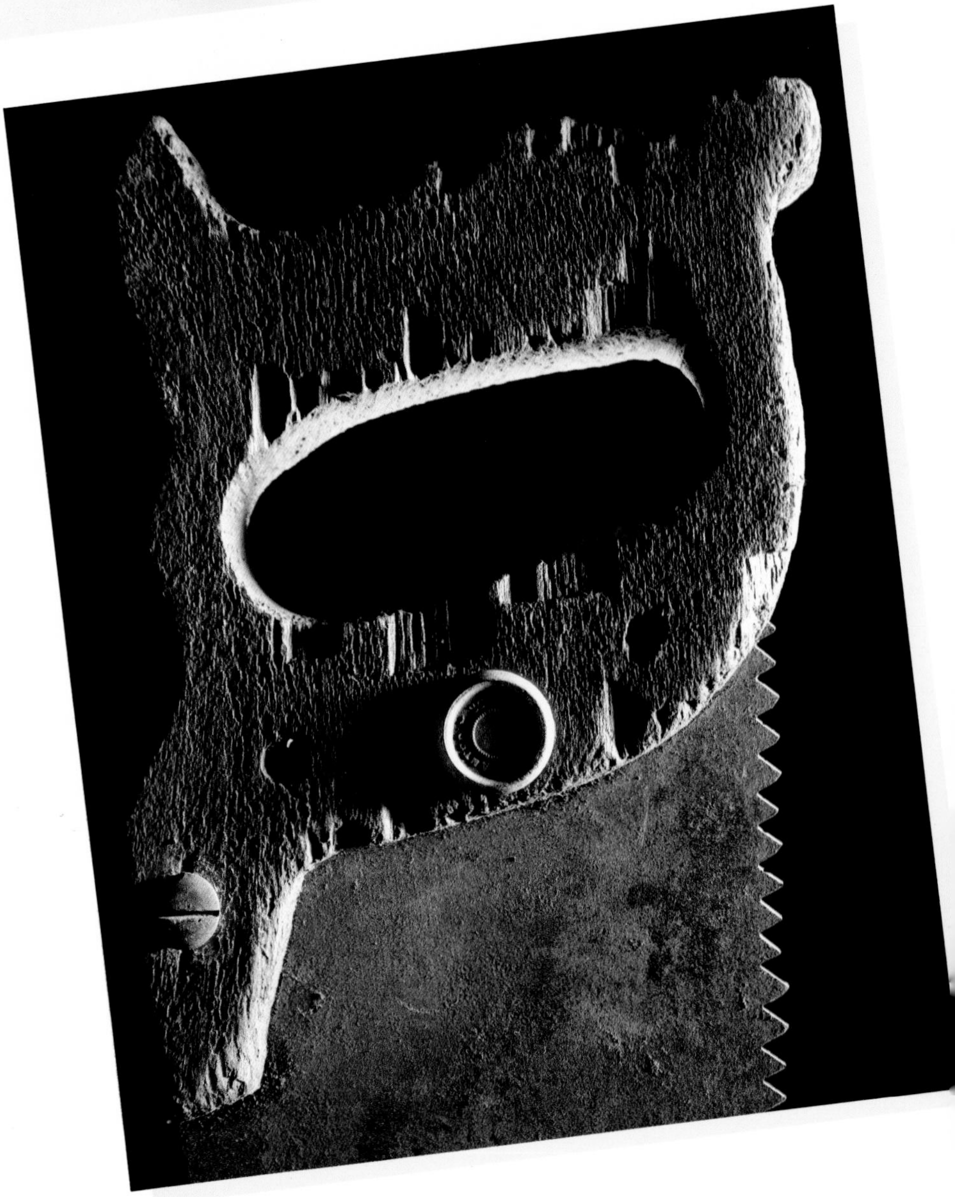

AKIS PRODUCTIONS

102 Railroad Avenue, Hackensack, NJ 07601 ◆ 201.342.8070 ◆ 201.342.8078

TRADITIONAL

NIKE

102 Railroad Avenue, Hackensack, NJ 07601 ◆ 201.342.8070 ◆ 201.342.8078

AKIS PRODUCTIONS

DIGITAL

DIGITAL

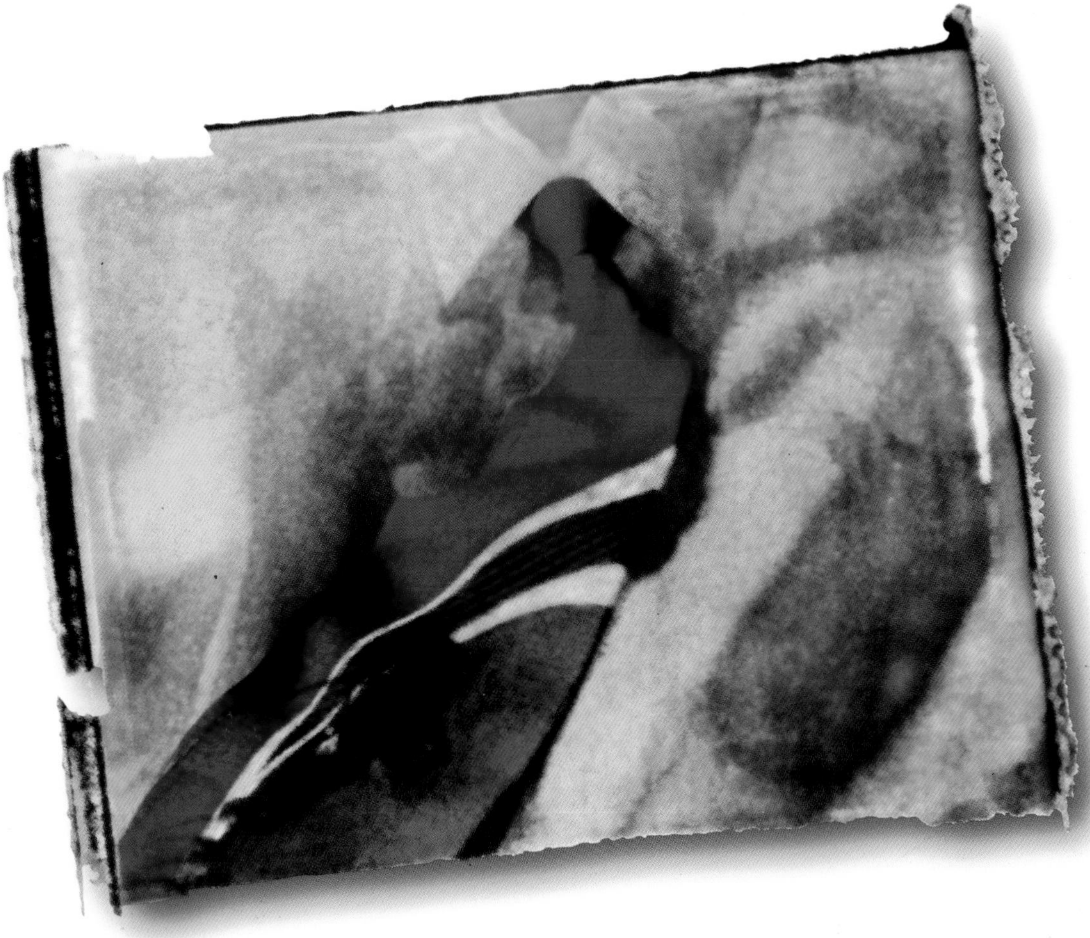

102 Railroad Avenue, Hackensack, NJ 07601 ◆ 201.342.8070 ◆ 201.342.8078

AKIS PRODUCTIONS

PETER OLSON

DNA

Clockwise:
American Institute of Graphic Arts: *Business Impact Poster*
Wyeth-Ayerst: *Biological Development Brochure*
Northeast Utilities: *Environmental Brochure*

SUITE 601 211 NORTH 13TH STREET PHILADELPHIA PA

215.972.8790

DAVID PRUITT

JOY
DE
JEAN PATOU
PARIS

212 684 8299

Martin Jacobs

59 West 19th Street New York, NY 10011 212 206-0941 FAX 212 206-0816

SMIRNOFF
OLIVE 'R TWIST.

SPARKY HAS RELIED ON A DELTA FAUCET FOR MOST OF HIS LIFE AND NEVER HAD A COMPLAINT.
DELTA
The way water is brought to life

REPRESENTED BY SANDI MOLLOD • PRINT • TELEVISION

212 • 758 • 1009

Weller & Water–
Wonderful™
SINCE 1849
SPECIAL RESERVE
90
PROOF
Old
90 Proof
W. L. Weller
SPECIAL RESERVE

User 2
User 1

M b I i L l N l E

ILL MILNE PHOTOGRAPHY 140 WEST 22ND STREET, NEW YORK, NY 10011 TELEPHONE 212•255•0710

REPRESENTATION LISA CICHOCKI

TONY CORDOZA
212 889 7022

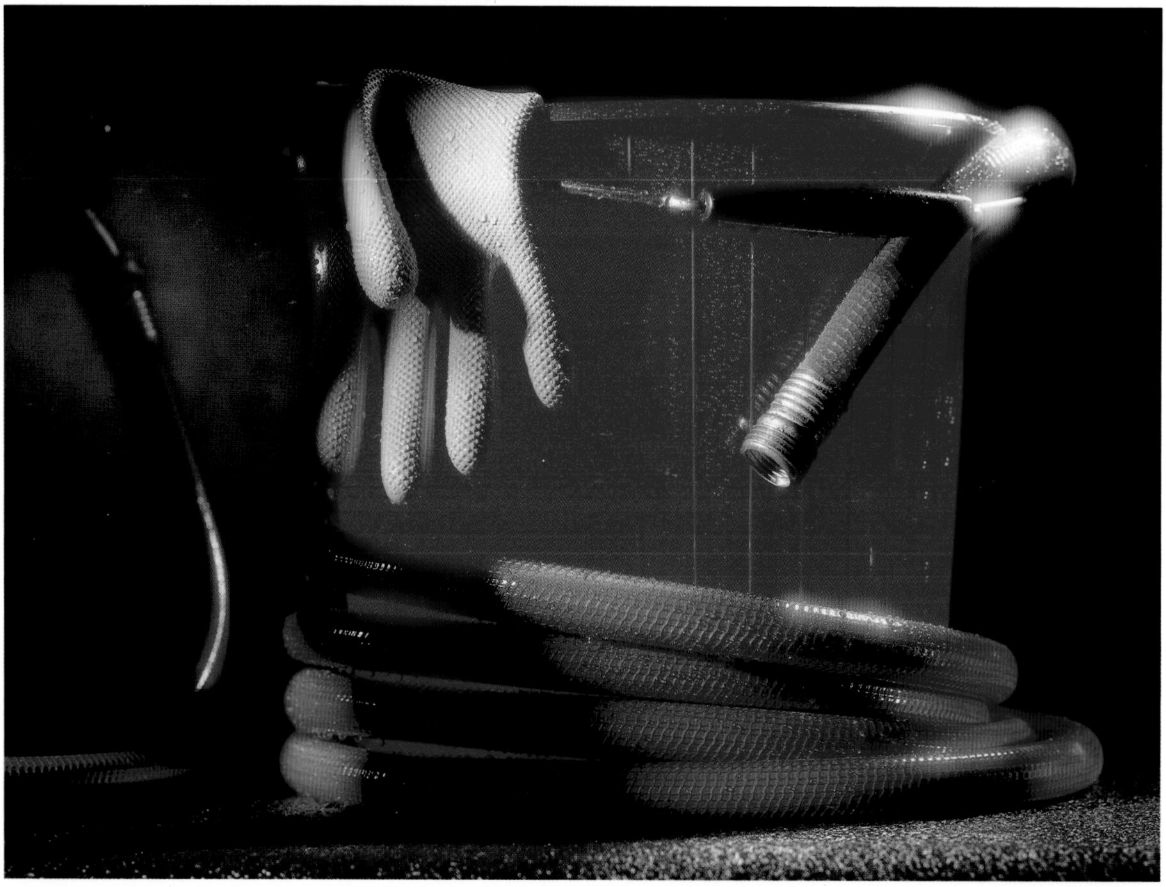

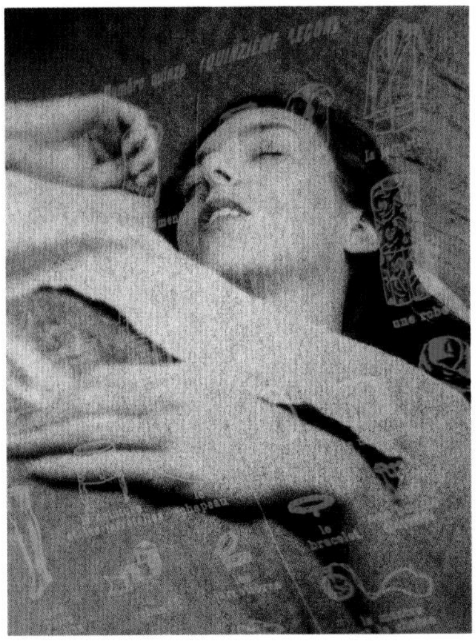

PASSPORT
Business Day

TELEPHONE

212.727.2493

FACSIMILE

212.727.2548

EARL RIPLING • PHOTOGRAPHY •

NYC NY 10011

33 W 17TH ST

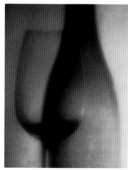

MITRAL

212-206-0429
EDWAR
212-20
EDWARD HOLLUB
JKL
5
PRS
7
ROXY

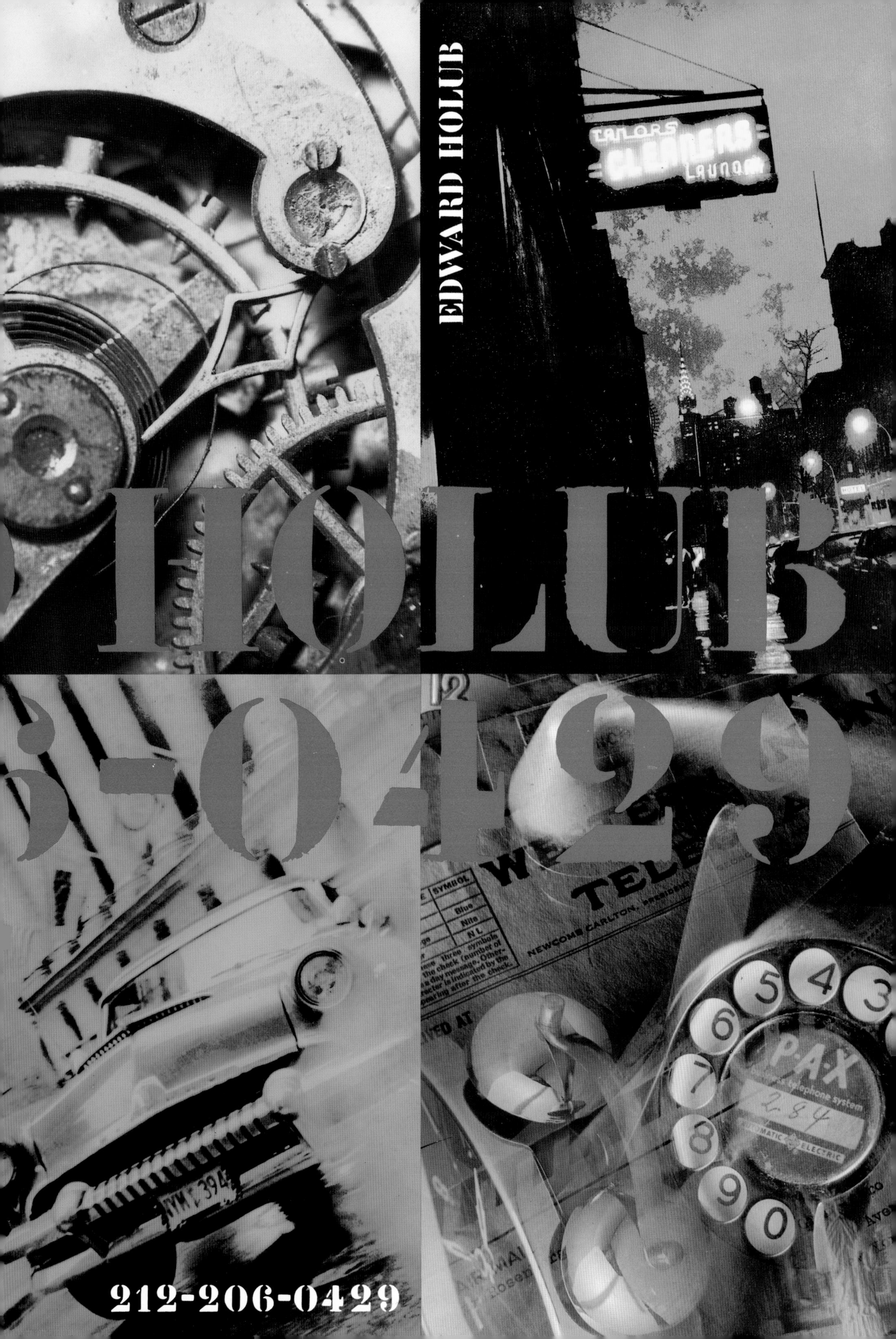
EDWARD HOLUB
CLEANERS
HOLUB
-0429
TEL
NEWCOMB CARLTON, PRESIDENT
P·A·X
212-206-0429

ETERNITY

perrier

SHARP

J A M E S   T   M U R R A Y

P H O T O G R A P H Y

WALL STREET JOUR
Dow Jones & Company, Inc.

REPRESENTED BY CAMERA ONE
62 WEST 45TH STREET NYC 10036
212...827 0500

PERRY ELLIS

LAYOUT DESIGN DARSHANA SHILPI

PETER JOHANSKY
212 • 242 • 7013

Niefield

Terry Niefield Studio/1123 Broadway/New York, NY 10010/212 686-8722

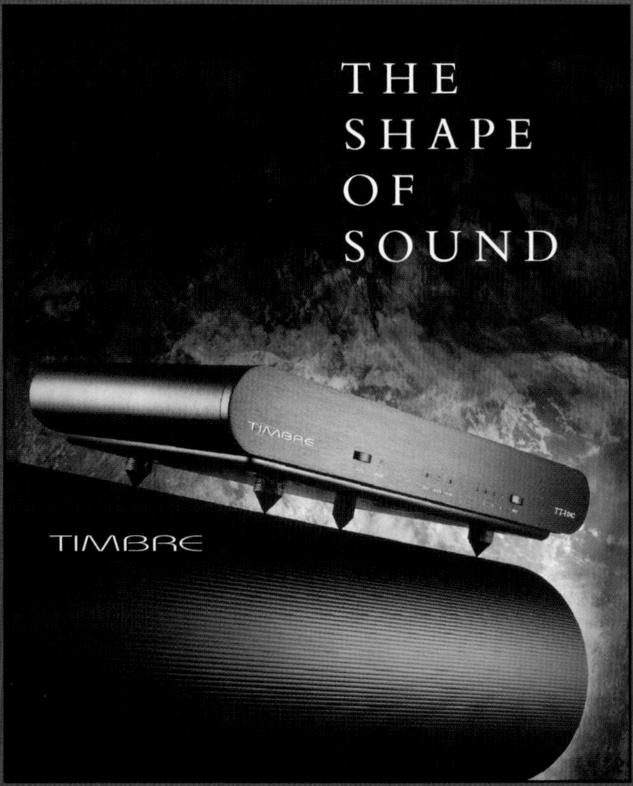
THE
SHAPE
OF
SOUND
TIMBRE

SONY
SONY
Color Video Printer
Mavigraph
STILL PERFECTION.

PARIS

rickburda

335 West 38th Street • Suite No. 7b • New York, NY 10018 • Telephone 212.971.9455

Jay Alan
Lefkowitz
212-929-1036

Chris Lysohir
Agent
212-741-3187

NEW ESSENTIALS
Hydrating Eye Cream
NET WT. .75 OZ./21 GMS

A.D: D. Collins

A.D: D. Frie

OGRUDEK

WEDNESDAY
ROLEX
OYSTER PERPETUAL
6

PHOTOGRAPHY

212·645·8008

L'ORÉAL
VISUELLE
Makeup Fluide
1.25 FL.OZ.

PFD PHOTOGRAPHY

Comtes de Champagne
TAITTINGER
ROSE
CHAMPAGNE 1983
BRUT

ESTÉE LAUDER
Time Zone Eyes
Ultra-Hydrating Complex

PAUL F. DANTUONO
433 PARK AVENUE SOUTH
NEW YORK, NY 10016
212-683-5778

M I C H A E L   M A Y O

56 WEST 22ND ST.
2 1 2 . 7 4 1 . 3 2 4 4
FAX 212.255.0389

BRAUN

R I C H A R D
L E V Y

Richard Levy Studio New York City 212 243 4220 Fax 212 243 624

SONY
f=5.5~66mm 1:1.6 ø52
12x
VARIABLE ZOOM
FOCUS
AUTO
video Hi8
CCD-VX3 Hi8™ Handycam® Pro Camcorder

presented by Arlene Vallon 212 980 1522 Fax 212 980 2881

Christopher Lawrence

STUDIO 212.807.8028 / FAX 212.366.9519
REPRESENTED BY *DARIO SACRAMONE* / 212.929.0487 / FAX 212.242.4429

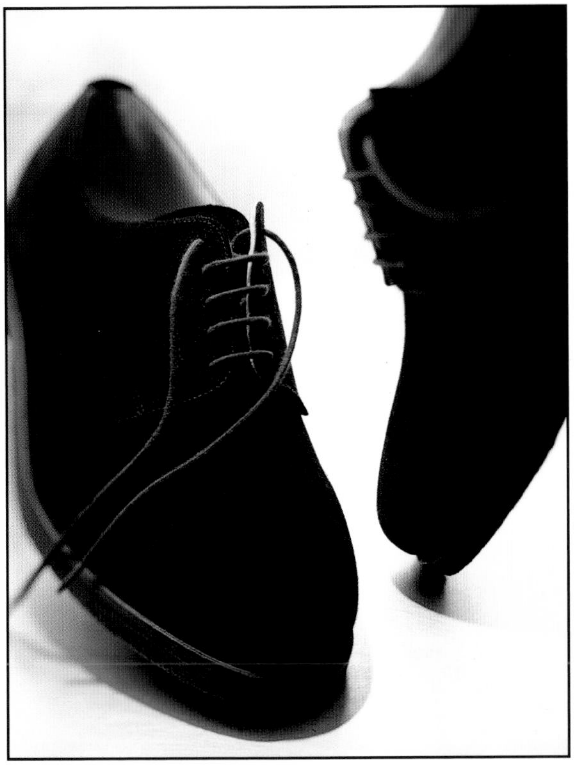

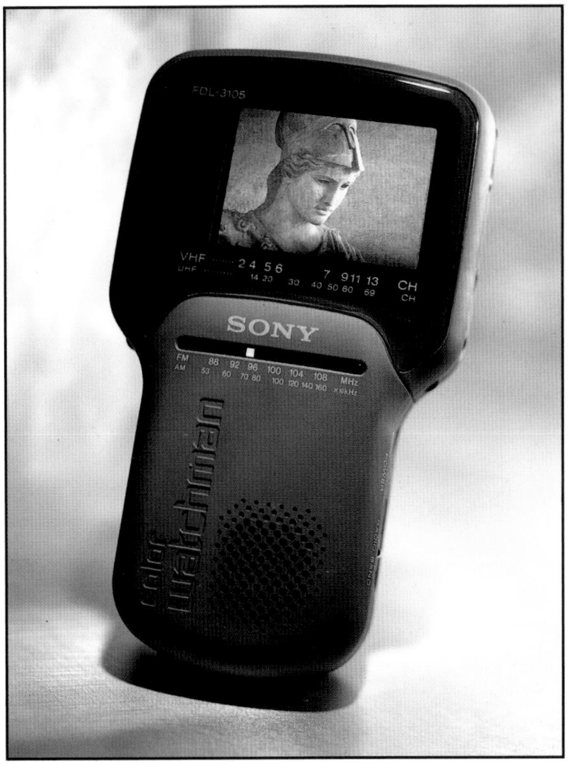
FDL-3105
SONY
Watchman

S T E F A N   H A G E N

R E P R E S E N T E D   B Y   O L I V E   H E A D

2 1 2 · 5 8 0   3 3 2 3

Walt Chrynwski

PHOTOGRAPHY

154 West 18 Street

New York, New York 10011

212.675.1906

Walt Chrynwski

PHOTOGRAPHY

Tektronix PHASER

154 West 18 Street

New York, New York 10011

212.675.1906

Ron

Brello
212 255 0041

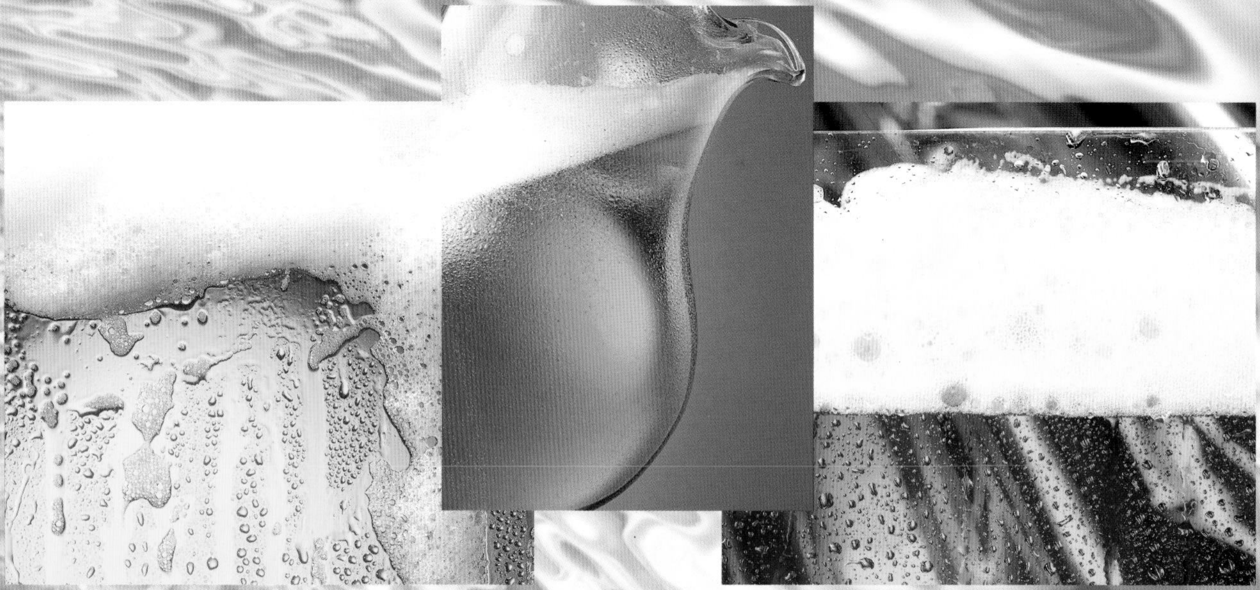

Carl Waltzer and the Scitex Leaf Digital Camera

SAVE THE DAY

Wines
of the
World

It's morning in the big city
and you've got a concept
that's aching for photography.
You are haunted by
evil voices from above.
"There's no time!"
"There's no money in the budget!"
"There's no way!"
Suddenly, a mysterious force
and great wisdom lead you to
Carl Waltzer and the
Scitex Leaf Digital Camera.
The shot is set up in the
fully equipped digital studio.
The shutter clicks.
In a matter of seconds
your shot is digitized
and ready for manipulation.
No polaroids.
No film and processing.
No scanning.
There's even time in the day
and money in the pocket for
a spectacular color proof
and separations.
With job well done,
you are on your merry way.
Carl Waltzer Digital Services
saves the day!

Carl WALTZER digital services inc.

212.475.8748

anon CLC 550 Cyclone Proofs • Iris 3024 Ink Jet Proofs • 3M Rainbow Proofs • 3M Match Print • Linotronic L300 • Scitex Dolev
citex Smart Scanner • Scitex Resolut RGB-CMYK • Full-service Photo Studio and Design Services • Call for a portfolio review.
873 Broadway New York City 10003 Fax 212.475.9359 Modem 212.475.9127